Elucidate

Editing by Ebook Launch
Book cover design by Ebook Launch
Book design and formatting by Reider Books
Illustrations by Exnier Benique

ISBN: 979-8-7732-3842-3 (Paperback)

Elucidate

The Way Out of Complex Problems

Rolando A. Berríos, PhD

This book is dedicated to my family —
Ana Cristina and Ana Ligia

"There are many reasonable ways to solve problems.
The skill at choosing an appropriate strategy
is best learned by solving many problems."

–George Pólya

Prologue

This book is about introducing systematic problem-solving to truly comprehend what is required to solve complex problem before you, your leaders, or your problem-solving team intuitively propose any solution.

Leaders and team members have different points of view and can be very persuasive, leading us to wrong corrective actions. This is worrying because their role is to provide guidance and find solutions to problems. So, taking the time and stepping back to understand the environment where the problem resides is the best start. Asking the following questions will help you think effectively about the problem. What is the problem we are trying to solve? What is the expected outcome? What is the impact of solving the problem? Who are the stakeholders? What is working well? What is the current information flow?

I have met many teams from successful service organizations that solve problems. These problem-solving teams range from engineering, project management, manufacturing production, finance, sales, human resources, quality, health-care clinic units, hospital emergency rooms, warehousing and distribution, supply chain, and data system analysis among others.

Some problems were complex, others not so complex. Every single problem-solving team I met had adopted a popular problem-solving approach. However, none of them followed through or even completed the phases because of lack of leadership, experience, or understanding how to sustain changes. I witnessed many times how leaders and problem-solving teams detoured their attention to what was next on their to-do list right after identifying a corrective action to solve the problem they were working on first.

As a problem-solver, you need to follow specific steps to solve problems—understanding the problem, applying a systematic method to analyze issues, implement solutions, and establish a program to sustain improvements.

This book helps you to elucidate what approach to take if you are new at applying techniques to solve problems. On the other hand, if you are a problem-solver practitioner, you might want to compare notes. I compiled a vast variety of basic tools and techniques into a logical approach to solve problems based on my experience applying them.

Problem-solving skills are a commodity these days, but we must be rigorous in solving problems the right way.

Here's how to start.

TABLE OF CONTENTS

INTRODUCTION   1

THINK IN SYSTEMS   11

UNDERSTANDING   21
    Map a Process   25
    Analyze the Process   28

SYSTEMATIC PROBLEM-SOLVING   31
    Define the Problem   36
    Conduct Analysis   37
    Collecting Data   39
        Work Sampling   41
        Time and Motion Study 47
    Data Cleansing   55
    Describing Data   57
    Illustrating Data   60
        Histogram   63
        Box and Whiskers Plot 67
        Scatter Plot   69
        Pareto Analysis   71
    Determining the Cause of the Problem   73
    Five Whys Analysis   75

Cause-and-Effect Diagram 77
Developing Corrective Actions 80
The Nominal Group Technique 83
The Delphi Technique 84
Monitoring Results 86

IMPROVEMENT 95
Waste Elimination 95
Continuous Improvement 98
5S 100
Responsibility Charting 103
Mistake-Proofing 105
Cost-Benefit Analysis 107

SUSTAINMENT 115
Standardization 116
Key Performance Indicators (KPIs) 119
Accountability 124

ROLE, ATTITUDE, BASIC SKILLS 127
Role 127
Attitude 130
Basic Skills 132

FINAL THOUGHTS 137

INTRODUCTION

In every organization I observe, the need to hire people with problem-solving skills continues to grow exponentially. Solving problems requires critical thinking, active listening, competency in analysis, and people management skills. Individuals who master these skills are engaged in a way that allows them to do their jobs better; therefore, the organization's performance improves. An army of problem-solvers will give a competitive advantage in any market, and provide infinite potential to any organization's customers.

Developing a systematic, problem-solving-based approach for operational excellence across an organization requires more than hiring highly qualified individuals. It requires an internal organizational structure that safely promotes critical thinking and creates an adaptable environment. To succeed, an organization must have an operational management system, fully supported by leadership, which prevents unproductive business behaviors from reemerging.

Leadership engagement is key to supporting any systematic improvement approach toward problem-solving. I have seen organizations develop unique approaches to solve problems, but I have seen many more that only give the *appearance* of having a systematic approach.

I have no doubt you, too, have seen these organizations. A commonly used approach is top-down management. In a top-down approach, leadership identifies a problem and assigns a project manager to deal with it. Then, leadership checks in for progress and intervenes if things are not moving forward or getting the desired results. Sadly, this approach denotes poor organizational design; leadership is inadequately connected and cannot give attention to critical issues. They then fail to understand their role in supporting a team's efforts toward overcoming problem-solving challenges. The phrase "paralysis of analysis" has become popular among leaders, and many use it to express frustration when a problem-solving initiative isn't moving at the right speed. For me, this is a symptom of the top-down approach. Leaders who continue using this kind of expression demonstrate total disconnection and lack of understanding concerning how to provide the right guidance and support to their teams. As a result, people disengage.

Employee engagement is key in any problem-solving or improvement initiative. I have met people assigned as part of a problem-solving effort who are clueless about their roles; they are actively disengaged. This is a complicated situation to deal with since a number of factors can influence people's level of engagement. However, in my experience, leaders should be encouraged to set expectations from the get-go, ensuring that the team understands all phases required to solve a problem, as well as the hard questions that need to be answered. When people understand the importance of their contribution to successfully solving a problem, they feel more connected to elucidating the problem they seek to solve.

This book is intended to provide a better understanding of what it takes to implement effective problem-solving strategies. Having an organization that aspires to or promotes a problem-solving culture requires one to leverage a systematic approach to solving complex problems for operational excellence. These days, where there are so many business competencies involved in developing new products and services, an emphasis on problem-solving can make a significant contribution and provide great advantage in transforming your business operations. There have been many studies and much research on different problem-solving or process improvement methods that I do not pretend to duplicate here. You can find many management improvement methodologies with the objective to systematically evaluate and identify what needs to be changed for the better. Such methodologies include Plan-Do-Check-Act (PDCA); Define, Measure, Analyze, Improve, Control (DMAIC); Kata; Observe-Orient-Decide-Act; and 8D, among others. However, I have taken some of the techniques and tools from various methodologies mentioned and applied them when needed.

My intention is merely to share what has worked for me in applying problem-solving techniques in various industries throughout my professional career. I succinctly give a basic understanding of those problem-solving phases that I consider the *must-do-can't-fail* to those who have some or no experience participating in a problem-solving initiative. Also, the reader will learn what to expect in each problem-solving phase to ensure better contribution, as well as guidance on how to support those leaders who must be involved in any given improvement effort. You might find nothing new here if you are a problem-solving or process improvement practitioner; nevertheless, you will enjoy how I organize the problem-solving approach and learn how this book can be of benefit to a problem-solver neophyte.

I have created a problem-solving road map, beginning with understanding the whole environment in which a problem resides. "Understanding" can be defined as a stage that helps us identify the main events within a process and how activities are connected to expected outcomes. This stage uses flow diagrams to help track down problems where they occur. A flow diagram must precisely depict all current activities, including possible gaps between people's perceptions of present situations. Developing a flow diagram allows us to capture necessary information regarding the problem-solving team's initial conditions; then we must determine the level of detail needed to analyze how the different activities or subprocesses impact one another, further clarifying the perceived gap.

The rationale for the understanding stage is to get good insights into the actual situation and identify potential areas for improvement manifesting as inefficiencies. Moreover, the understanding stage gives us the opportunity to identify any externality as the potential cause of a problem. I have worked with problem-solving teams that isolate the problem from the rest of the operation, excluding other units, divisions, people, space areas, and even information technology systems that may have a direct link to the problem. Therefore, it is highly desirable to understand the environment of the problem, plotting all dimensions into 360 degrees. Think of this stage as a law enforcement team that is assigned to analyze a crime scene: every single piece of evidence counts.

A systematic, problem-solving approach involves closing the perceived gap between a current situation and a desired goal. The approach discussed in this book follows the A3 report. A3 is the size of a piece of paper. Back in the 1960s, the quality management team from Toyota Motors (the automotive manufacturer) used an 11" x 17" piece of paper as a standardized form to document all problem-solving phases. This was their systematic approach to expose problems as they occurred, and it ensured a proper problem definition—including measurable gap—acknowledging problem impact, problem analysis, root-cause analysis, corrective actions, and a validation system.

For instance, my experience in applying the A3 approach to a health-care setting includes closing the gaps in the patient fall prevention system. I used the A3 approach to address strategic patient fall preventions with executives: *"Why are patient fall events increasing?"* I also facilitated discussion around daily patient fall prevention tactics with physicians, nurses, and clinical technicians, using starting points such as, *"Why did staff responsiveness time to patient-initiated call lights and bed alarms drop?"* Patient falls are one of the most common harm events in health-care clinical units. By applying the A3 approach, the health-care staff involved in the system strengthening of patient fall prevention initiative successfully demonstrated patient readmission avoidance and a 15% improvement in service essentials scores for patient satisfaction.

Having a systematic approach helps organizations make deliverable decisions, ensuring that relevant information has been analyzed and alternatives defined. This approach also requires that specific steps be completed before the team moves to the next phase of problem-solving.

First, the team acknowledges that there is a problem that needs to be solved. They describe the problem to be addressed, focusing on the problem without advocating potential solutions. Second, the team identifies the people closest to the work to solve problems; these are individuals who can contribute the most value through sharing their knowledge and providing insight. It is beneficial to work with those who have observed the problem firsthand. Third, the team must seek out various pieces of information related to the problem identified. They then analyze the information gathered and determine potential causes of a problem. They should dive into potential causes to understand their origins. Next, the team brainstorms for potential corrective actions to tackle the root cause. They assess each corrective action by seeking additional information or data, determining level of effort, calculating costs associated for implementation, and identifying the risk impact. After this step, they decide and plan what corrective action to implement first. Then, they get a consensus from the leader on the implementation plan. Finally, the team implements one or two corrective actions at a time. They monitor the results and validate the outcomes, adjusting and adapting the action plan as needed based on the obtained results.

The problem-solving team should seek strategies to ensure they can adapt to their changing environment, maintaining the adjustments in order to remain competitive in the market. One leading strategy is waste elimination. "Waste" refers to nonvalue-added activities present within any given business process—those that are unable to impact the production of a good, or the way a service is provided. Customers are not willing to pay for nonvalue-added activities. Identifying waste will require paying attention to those activities or tasks directly related to time, equipment, labor, supplies, or information systems that negatively impact inventory, motion, processing, overproduction, waiting, transportation, human capital, and defects.

Each improvement initiative is not a one-time occurrence, but rather a continuous event moving the organization toward excellence. Identifying and eliminating activities that do not add value to your business operations, while implementing corrective actions, will not occur overnight. These waste activities will pop up while you continue adapting to changes, and you must have a strategy in place to bring waste to an absolute minimum over time.

Similarly, the 5S Principle helps improvement initiatives because it allows one to effectively organize work areas and operational procedures. The implementation of 5S is conducive to visual control and contributes to reducing waste in many ways. The "5S" refers to five terms that start with letter S: sort, set in order, shine, standardize, and sustain.

First, you sort to eliminate unnecessary items in the work area, or eliminate unnecessary steps in the case of business processes. Second, you organize whatever remains from sorting and arrange those items neatly. You should maintain a place for everything and keep everything in its place. Shine is the third cleansing aspect of 5S; this is a form of quality inspection using precision and finer processing technologies. Fourth, you must standardize the workplace or business process by defining the most reliable practices. Finally, you sustain the 5S program by identifying and defining metrics to constantly measure performance, empowering people to make changes for the better.

You may also incorporate some other improvement strategy such as a Kaizen. A Kaizen event leads your team and organization to the habit of constantly thinking about how to improve. Kaizen is a way of thinking with the goal to improve for the better by engaging teams in conversations and activities to reach a desired goal. This engagement must be continuous; in other words, it never ends. There are qualitative benefits, such as staff engagement, customer satisfaction, safe work environment, improved compliance, better access to information, communication, and knowledge management. Similarly, quantitative benefits can be identified, such as elimination of inefficient processes, faster response to market needs, increased profitability, and better quality of product and services outcomes.

Benefits or costs are not necessarily obvious at first. They require thoughtful evaluation and an understanding of what is necessary to reach a goal. This is because many hidden benefits and costs do not stand out just by having a conversation, mapping, or analyzing data related to an area of desired improvement. Benefit-cost analysis is a tool that can be utilized to evaluate the pros and cons of any given improvement initiative, and it can complement a decision-making process. Since a team must decide whether to proceed with the implementation of corrective actions given other options of benefits and costs, a game changer can certainly result from this analysis.

A responsibility matrix is another tool included in the improvement toolbox that may benefit problem-solving efforts.

It is a permanent mechanism that helps leaders to pursue excellence throughout an organization in which individuals are assigned to specific tasks. For instance, a responsible, accountable, consulted, and informed (RACI) matrix is a set of rules in a responsibility assignment system; you have people assigned to every task and decision included in the improvement plan, and there are defined owners for each step. This system brings communicative structure and clear expectations when it comes to the task of assigning roles to individuals within the improvement initiative.

A problem-solving initiative depends on empowering people to make changes and giving them the tools and skills they need to improve the business. They need a fully equipped toolbox to support a structured, problem-solving approach, and they must have a good grasp of the current situation facing the problem-solving team. This requires a shift in leadership thinking, including the allocation of resources with appropriate accountability. It also means that leaders need to trust the knowledge and judgment of the people who have been involved from day one, while still assessing the actions required for improvement. The objective here is to explain a systematic approach to solving problems along with different analysis methodologies, while referring to specific examples.

Embedding a problem-solving approach in your organization requires a new narrative from leaders. It also necessitates a meaningful role for frontline staff, who elucidate problems so that improvement activity is aligned with what they most need and value.

THINK IN SYSTEMS

I n my experience, I have come across many smart and committed individuals who are skilled in tools and methods to solve problems. They have faced challenges when it comes to analyzing problems in areas such as business-critical processes, staff productivity, manufacturing operations, production, sales, finance transactions, information flow, communication, information systems integration, supply chain, or human resources. All these individuals were assigned to address a situation that impeded a team, unit, division, or organization to get the work done effectively. *What was their task?* To solve a problem. *What was their main challenge?* The thinking process required to solve a problem. A common denominator I noticed is that most of them are surprisingly unaware of the thinking process they use to solve problems. When they are called to evaluate a problem, they feel that they must come up with an answer, and it must be the right answer. Their tendency is to immediately come up with a solution, putting it at the beginning of the process, when what they need to start with is a corrective action once they've reached the end of the thinking process.

This tendency to try to find a solution right away may be motivated by the fact that people often have different expectations or opinions on issues and goals, and consequently, their potential solutions differ as well. Therefore, without a structured thinking process that keeps the team on the same page, they risk running in different directions and not addressing the source of the problem.

I have also noticed a common thinking process toward complex problem-solving. First, the team describes the consequences caused by the problem. Then, an actionable plan is developed after ideating on possible solutions based on information on hand. Next, they implement the most suitable solution.

Let's think through this approach before moving forward. Complex problem-solving requires brainstorming potential solutions to develop an actionable plan. The outcome is just a plan to document what needs to be done; it is a reminder of which corrective actions need to happen and when. Also, the action plan serves as a communication and collaboration tool for problem solvers. After reviewing these plans, I concluded that they were well structured, including dependencies, which tells me that a team of problem solvers reviewed all the issues logically and identified all the relevant issues and constraints. However, were they able to identify the problem's root causes? Were they working on actions that have an impact on the gap created by the consequences of the problem? Bottom line: were they working on the right thing?

Teams assume they have all the information to solve a problem. They address why a problem occurred and they think they know the cause of the problem, but they don't validate any of their conclusions. When teams overlook the obvious or the not-so-obvious, they unwittingly or lazily accept blind decision-making as an adequate countermeasure to a problem. However, problem solvers may have forgotten to look for causal relationships, or they may have forgotten to do something as simple as observe and listen to people who may routinely deal with the problem firsthand.

Many times, teams fail to determine the root cause, devoting unnecessary time and resources to focusing on handling the signs rather than zeroing in on the real problem. A *sign* is an indication of the possibility that a problem *might* occur rather than a real problem itself. For example, being overweight is an indication that an individual is facing health issues, but gaining excessive weight is not the real problem. Most people will work to resolve this sign by changing their diet, but has the real problem been addressed? Here we need to have a more in-depth conversation. Maybe there are existing preconditions, genetics, physical inactivity, insulin resistance, psychological factors, and medications, among others. Many details need to be discussed if the individual wants to find the actual problem.

How About Thinking in Systems?

The problem-solving process requires a deep understanding of the system where problems reside, and the ability to leverage the behavior of interconnected elements, activities, human factors, and information. There is a reason for this: for every problem we face, there are input variables, elements interacting with each other, and desired and undesired outcomes led by a great effort of resources. A problem-solving approach allows us to understand a system's behavior through the identification of nonvalue-added activities, trends, and events that may be the cause of further effects in a cyclical pattern.

Let me start this journey by shifting our thinking pattern from *how* to *what*. We are trained to think of solutions, and some people include the *think-out-of-the-box* motto in their thought process. This is the generalized expectation from a problem solver. Therefore, problem solvers limit their thought processes to *how* they are going to solve the problem, instead of thinking about the purpose of a solution to a simple and fast "what-if" statement. We usually don't stop to think and develop a simple *what-if-then* statement. As time goes on, and we evaluate the outcome of our decision, we begin to make sense of the importance of putting thought into the problem that we are trying to solve as opposed to what the outcome of our actions will be. The goal here is to develop a habit of thinking in a systematic way by focusing on the system, its purpose, and the environment where the problem resides. In other words, it is a thinking process that enables analysis about the way a problem is affecting the system's interrelated fundamental parts, as well as an understanding of how the system will be impacted over time. The appeal of using a problem-solving approach is that it is effective for solving the most difficult types of problems in complex systems.

What Is a System?

The International Council on Systems Engineering provides a general definition of a system as an arrangement of parts or elements that together exhibit behavior or meaning that the individual constituents do not. Systems can be either physical or conceptual, or a combination of both. For the purposes of this book, I have interpreted a system as an organized collection of parts or subprocesses that are integrated to accomplish an overall goal, for instance, a natural system, human body system, social system, solar system, government systems, health-care systems, education systems, satellite system, Department of Defense Aviation Command and Control System, and Ground Combat System, among others. Every system mentioned has all their components interrelated in some way. Without such interdependencies, there is no system, only a bunch of independent parts.

A health-care system considers various aspects involved in patient acuity to meet health needs to the population they serve. Understanding how these aspects depend on one another will help with a problem-solving approach to investigating the interconnectivity of all elements necessary for proper functionality—health-care unit, patient-clinician interaction, patient's family support—to promote better health service at a lower cost. Basically, we try to gain a better understanding of a system by reflecting on the interaction of the crucial factors that define it.

Another example is the Aqua Satellite, a joint project between the United States, Japan, and Brazil. This mission collects large data sets about Earth's water cycle, including evaporation from the oceans, water vapor in the atmosphere, clouds, precipitation, soil moisture, sea ice, land ice, and snow cover on land and ice. Aqua is focused on the multidisciplinary study of Earth's interrelated processes; therefore, the information gathered by the integration of six science instruments yields data to improve atmospheric studies of weather, climate, and other aspects of the atmosphere. Atmospheric scientists use Aqua as a tool to develop reports and forecasts from their analysis of weather and climate that could be critical to areas of economic development.

Both examples, health-care systems and Aqua Satellite, are complex systems for a specific purpose in our day-to-day lives. So, thinking in systems is not stepping back to evaluate the big picture, but rather comprehending what the system has to do, and the priorities and consequences associated with it. This helps us understand how the problem-solving approach fits into the system (process or service) and what consequences the solutions will have on the overall performance of the system. There is a need to keep balance between solutions that add value to a process or service and solutions that obstruct the flow of work. Value-added solutions help individuals produce consistent outputs more efficiently with a minimum of defects or errors. Temporary or Band-Aid solutions do not solve problems; they are just easily profited-off ideas that may offer superficial remedies, but usually end up creating even more problems of their own. It is easy to lower your guard and get into a thinking mode based on the premise that corrective actions are unwelcome, challenging, require dramatic changes, and hold people accountable. Changing ingrained habits, and in some cases decades of doing things the same way, requires both desire and cognitive change.

The highest priority is establishing sustainable change across the organization and project. Doing so allows for integration with the current culture, processes, and practices. Ultimately, in system-based thinking, the main objective is to understand how long-term process improvement strategies impact business goals and the success of the organization.

Where Do We Begin?

Directors and managers need to identify a senior leader or executive sponsor responsible for the success of the process improvement initiative. The sponsor needs to provide the vision and ensure that the process of improving goals is aligned with the overall organization strategy. All director and manager levels need to support the vision and provide the team responsible for improving the processes with appropriately skilled and trained individuals.

Before conducting a problem-solving event, show the sponsor and improvement team some typical cases of how problem-solving has been successfully implemented in your work area. Describe the fundamentals of problem-solving and set expectations in terms of goals and milestones, ensuring that they are widely communicated and universally understood.

To this point, the problem-solving team must be convinced that the sponsor has a solid argument for undertaking an improvement initiative. Next, you should walk the team through the systematic approach to such a program, and cover key components of the problem-solving approach.

The key components are:

+ Understanding—Staff should be able to analyze process activities they perform daily and conduct a discussion on whether targets were met.

- Systematic problem-solving—Adapt a structured method that allows a robust analysis to discover opportunities to improve.
- Improvement—Optimization and standardization of processes once corrective actions are proved to deliver the intent, meeting outcome expectations.
- Sustainment—Strategy to ensure human behavior changes as improvements occur to avoid reverting to the way a work or process was done before improvements.

By adopting problem-solving skills, we become more flexible and resilient in dealing with broken complex systems. Because solving challenges can limit the ability to efficiently handle a situation, it is essential to follow methods and techniques available in an individual's tool kit in order to solve those problems. In a world where we constantly face challenges, disruptions, and broken processes, the best options are creativity and insights. For instance, when working on a problem, organizations must constantly refresh their problem-solving team in order to find capable people with the required skill set who are the best fit for their organization's problem-solving objectives.

The purpose of a problem-solving road map is to use a thinking process as an approach to making small improvements over time. A road map offers individuals an established tool for assessing problems, sustaining potential corrective actions based on their level of skills, and managing the uncertainty of complex decision-making. This approach is effective for maintaining gains and the improvement individuals need to work continuously. This road map provides guidance on the necessary steps and tools needed to implement problem-solving methodologies to help eliminate nonvalue-added activities. It is built on the legacies of W. Edwards Deming and Walter A. Shewhart's management method (used in business for the continual improvement of processes): the Plan-Do-Check-Act (PDCA). This method is applicable to all types of work across all business units, and is a simple version of Shewhart's original methodological proposals around scientific inference. Unfortunately, I have seen many problem solvers underestimating its simplicity, which leads them to one solution: ignoring the need to test the cycle with experiments.

A renewed focus on the human behavior side of change increases the likelihood that efforts to improve an operational system will succeed in the short term and be scaled and sustained over time. Several industries and government agencies highlight the significance of having problem solvers who can successfully deal with complex problems. This road map is intended to suit up individuals with knowledge and tools to understand the system or process where a problem occurs, analyze the problem, conduct root cause analysis, define a corrective action plan, monitor progress, streamline processes, and sustain changes. To achieve the goal of the road map, four holistic strategies that require skills and experience are developed. These four holistic strategies are based on problem-solving best practice, and are: (1) understanding, (2) systematic problem-solving, (3) improvement, (4) sustainment.

UNDERSTANDING

To clarify a process and define the actions in its current state, individuals should be able to understand and analyze activities performed daily. Understanding is the first stage in the road map that helps individuals identify the sequence of the main events within a process of delineating activities, redundancies, process holdups (bottlenecks), non-value-added activities, people and department interrelations, information technology that supports operations, information, and data flow, and how all activities are connected with the expected outcomes. Moreover, determining supplies, materials, equipment, human resources, and methods as well as the drivers for each activity is key during this exercise.

This stage uses flow diagrams to identify each action within a system or process. Mapping activities to understand a process can also help to track down problems where they occur. When developing a flow diagram, consider the amount of information needed, how it will be used, and by whom. This will help the team determine the level of detail to include. While mapping a process, individuals must consider the activities' attributes within a process, such as human resources, equipment, supplies, method or work instructions, and cycle time to complete each task. Each of these is key information that will enable the team to map the flow with a complete understanding of potential problems, such as miscommunication, lack of information and upper management support, team collaboration, procedures variation, defects, tool failure, idle time, machine or equipment downtime, process handovers, and accountability. A flow diagram is a versatile tool during the first stage of this road map. Its process should be initiated via agreeing on the start and end steps of the process and what level of information is required. After completing a first draft, decide with the team if further process details are required to gain more insights and better understanding.

Individuals must start by identifying the processes for the products or services from the starting and finishing points. At the beginning of the diagraming effort, an as-is (current state) process flow helps the team to understand the actual situation of business processes. The team may benefit by assessing this current state with a desired long-term goal of what the business process will look like in the future (future state). Begin with simple data collection of expected outcomes. Then, a simple flowchart with only a few steps should be built, followed by subflow diagrams with more detail into the process. To enable a process overview is recommended in order to follow the supplier, input, process, output, and customer (SIPOC) approach. This process allows for a high-level understanding among process stakeholders of key processes. SIPOC is a high-level diagram documented in the form of a table that helps one visualize a process and its influences. This visualization helps the users identify relevant steps of the process and supports scoping a process mapping initiative. The term *supplier* could refer to a vendor, a third party, a department, a team, or a staff member that supplies input into a process. Define the inputs and critical steps in the process, then identify the expected outputs and the external or internal customer who would benefit from the process designed to provide a product or service. After completing the SIPOC exercise, a more specific flow diagram can be developed; it should depict what and who are responsible or accountable for performing key steps.

Let's assume that you are interested in assembling a mountain bike. Here (Figure 1) is a SIPOC showing a high-level process that identifies who supplies all bike parts and tools needed, the inputs necessary for the assembly operation, the assembly steps, the expected outcome of each step, and who would benefit or consume a fully functional mountain bike.

A process map is a management tool to blueprint the flow of business steps and information in a process using graphic symbols. Processes that are desired to be assessed or improved should be measured and analyzed. At this point, be sure to expand the steps listed under "Processes" in the SIPOC exercise, but don't get confused as to how to complete those steps. Just focus on *what* is happening and not *how* it happens. It is critical here to understand the information flow, people/team/department interactions, steps, interconnections, and handovers. This information can provide some insight or symptoms of challenges and/or pain points. Swim-lane diagrams (Figure 2) are useful tools to depict cross-functional flows and detail the subprocess responsibilities in a process. They are also used to group subprocesses according to responsibilities and accountabilities of certain resources, roles, or departments.

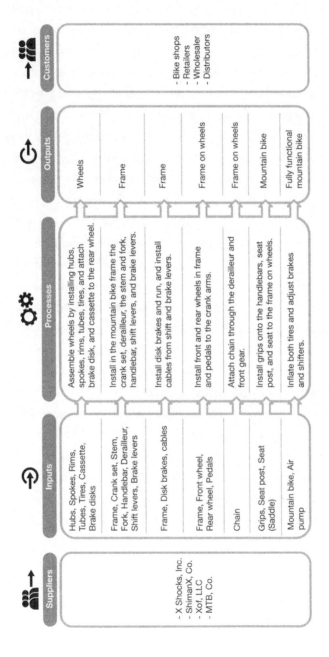

Figure 1: SIPOC for mountain bike assembly process
Diagram used to get team members to understand the process

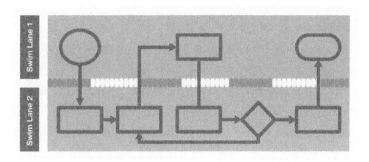

Figure 2: Swim-lane diagram

A more in-depth flow diagram is possible by data gathering and transforming data and information into a visual representation documenting how a process occurs at a transactional level. It is important to include information on how the work is undertaken for subprocesses so that decisions, bottlenecks, action flow, nonvalue-added activities, cycle times, delays, and duplication of efforts can be identified.

Map a Process

The following steps are key to mapping a process:

1. Pick a cross-functional team.
2. Identify operational processes that drive the business objectives and goals.
3. Select a mapping technique. Different process maps range and depict levels of detail from planning steps, activities, tasks, documents, roles, interactions, and outcomes.

Flowchart: A diagram that uses specific symbols to help organize your thoughts to get a desired outcome (see Figure 3). The basic symbols in flowcharts are circle (start point and page connector), rectangle (process), diamond (decision), oval (end point), and arrows (direction of flow connecting symbols). The diagram must depict a step-by-step process, including key information and data, to understand how a process operates. The problem-solving team must focus on one process at a time when developing a flowchart to be concise and to facilitate analysis without losing clarity. I consider flowcharts to be powerful tools that keep both the problem-solving team and process stakeholders fully engaged.

Value Stream Mapping: A process improvement technique to reveal the current situation of a business process, which is used as a baseline to design the ideal future state by depicting production and information flow differentiating between value-added and nonvalue-added activities.

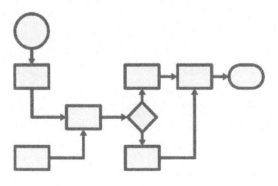

Figure 3: Flowchart

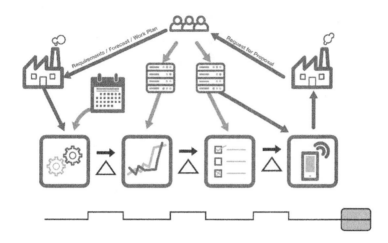

Figure 4: Value stream map

4. Observe the current process. After the first draft, spend time observing and walking through the current process, ensuring all key activities are captured and depicted more accurately.
5. Be sure to discover and identify subprocesses that support the main process.
6. Understand why each activity is done.
   a. Do they relate to nonvalue-added activities?
   b. Do the activities vary each time they are performed?
   c. Does variation, if any, affect quality?
   d. Is there any bottleneck or slow-down activity or task?
   e. Is there any similarity/redundancy between activities?
   f. If any similarity, can the activities be combined?
   g. If any similarity, is there any specialization or skill applied?

7. Document all the activities, tasks, and sub-tasks observed.
8. Draw the final draft. Arrange the sequence of activities recorded, and depict the process exactly as observed.

By mapping the whole process, the problem-solving team can visualize the connection between production flow and information flow. This exercise can be done in a conference room, but more importantly, it is for the improvement team to physically see and understand how each activity/task is really done. Also, perform a process walk-through for gathering process data, such as lead time, bottlenecks, work in progress, and cycle time.

Analyze the Process

Process analysis involves reviewing the attributes of a process, including activities, tasks, inputs, outputs, procedures, decisions, controls, process stakeholders, information flow, data sources, data, and information technologies to verify process accuracy and to judge how well a process works. After that review, the team may decide on changes to improve the current process. The following two steps may help the team to identify opportunities for improvement to optimize subprocesses, save lead time, lower costs, or minimize process variances.

Step 1: Review the flow by examining each task. Are the tasks documented in the right symbol? Does the sequence of the tasks follow a logical flow? Can you determine who is accountable to execute each task? Is it clear what must be accomplished in each task? What is the expected outcome for each task?

Step 2: Identify potential areas for improvements. Pay close attention to those activities or tasks that are ambiguous, unclear, uncertain, or lack information, and fix errors. Typically, processes with numerous errors have many reviews/inspections. These errors often are passed on to other process stakeholders who correct them without feedback to the error.

1. *Bottlenecks.* Points in the process that occur when workloads arrive too early/too quickly to handle, causing delays and higher process lead time.
2. *Process variability:* Activities or tasks that are not standardized, causing each person to execute in multiple ways, resulting in inconsistent outcomes.
3. *Weak links.* The connection or handoff between activities is not working properly, causing the process to operate with incorrect information and data, thereby weakening the remaining activities within the process.

The value of analyzing the current state map exercise is its practicality: it includes all the steps through the operation and management processes, identifying where the nonvalue-added activities reside. Also, it includes an overall setting for a common understanding of *what* and *how* a system or process is performed, which helps the team identify areas for improvement. Ultimately, this process allows products or service activities to flow through with the minimum deviation possible. Next, conduct problem-solving exercises based on improvement priorities and overall impact to the organization to make sense of the complex situation in which a problem occurs.

SYSTEMATIC PROBLEM-SOLVING

Individuals constantly face changes at work and continually confront a growing body of information. In my experience, much of the information is invalid or irrelevant to their operations. It is important to know how to sort and classify information to choose the part that is valid for analysis. Problem-solving exercises can apply a variety of approaches for unforeseen changes.

For example, if someone is asked to find the area of a storage room that has a rectangular shape, then this is a straightforward problem to solve. To solve this problem, you need to know the numerical value of the length and the width of the rectangle along with the unit of measurement, such as inches, feet, yards, kilometers, or miles. Proceed to apply the formula to find the area of a rectangle that is equal to the length multiplied by the width ($A = L \times W$). This is an analytical and standard exercise that requires direct measurement with specific length units. In general, the situation involves closing a gap in unknown information where the goal of finding the area of a storage room requires at least a specific solution.

There are other instances in which solving a problem by a decision-making process is required. We start this process by defining what event in a node is desired versus an event that is not desired. Then, from the first node, branches are developed based on possible outcomes; these lead to other nodes that drive additional possible outcomes. Let's develop a decision tree based on the classic weather forecast example, applying conditional probabilities or probabilities of an event. For instance, an individual is managing multiple tasks in a project, and the critical path is at risk, putting a hard completion date in jeopardy. The individual is responsible for facility infrastructure and maintenance. One building requires the exterior to be painted by a contractor; however, the individual knows that the weather forecast during the painting calls for a 50% chance of rain.

Starting from Node One—paint now versus postpone—there are two options: rainy or sunny, both a 50% chance. The rain option has some different possible outcomes. There are subnodes under the rain option that lead to four different possible outcomes. Similarly, the sunny option has subnodes leading to different outcomes. The benefit of this exercise is that all possible outcomes are known and considered. *How should the individual proceed with the information given?* First, the individual prioritizes these and figures out which is the best outcome—so, a basic conditional probability formula is required (see Figure 5).

The probability decision tree diagram helps determine if painting during the current period is possible or not. It will help the individual to determine what and how it can be done, and what else is required to make these things happen.

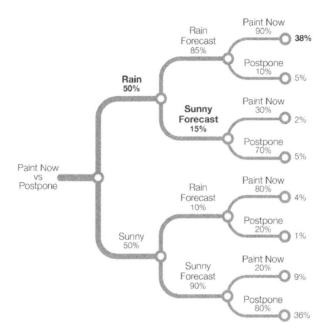

Figure 5: Decision tree
Decision tree example for painting activity based upon today's weather conditions.

In this case, a decision-making process was applied as part of the problem-solving process, where decision-making was used to choose among multiple possible solutions. There is a 38% chance of getting the painting job done, given that the weather forecast says that there is a 15% chance of a sunny day even when a rainy day is forecast.

These two previous analytical examples can be used to drive the discussion or to design a mathematical algorithm that provides the best choice. It allows an individual to define the course of actions based on probabilities, cost, or benefits.

There is also an inference approach applying a root cause analysis. This is an exercise that allows the users to discuss why and how a problem happens in order to determine corrective actions to prevent the same problems from happening again. This approach can use a combination of different tools and different methods. The most common is the five whys (5Ws) exercise. Regardless of the tools or methods used, the key to being successful while conducting a root cause analysis is the ability to have a thorough conversation with the team to break down all components and elements within the system and analyze the factors that contribute to an issue. There are many examples available of how to apply a root cause analysis. Let's pick one well-known 5Ws example: monument deterioration.

A monument is deteriorating rapidly, so the administration would like to know why and how this is happening. An individual was hired to serve as a facilitator to a problem-solving team, and they decided to conduct a root cause analysis applying the 5Ws approach. The analogy behind the 5Ws approach is that after the fifth time asking why, the team will reach the root cause. Ninety percent of the time, that is not the case. The facilitator initiated the exercise by asking the first "why" question.

Facilitator: *Why is the monument deteriorating?*

Team concludes: Because of the high content of chemicals in the cleaning products used to maintain the monument.

Facilitator: *Why are cleaning products with a high content of chemicals needed?*

Team concludes: To clean the bird droppings off the monument.

Facilitator: Why are there bird droppings on the monument?

Team concludes: Because there is a constant presence of spiders around the monument, which are a food source for birds.

Facilitator: Why is there a constant presence of spiders around the monument?

Team concludes: Because there are insects around the monument at dusk, which are a food source to spiders.

Facilitator: Why are insects drawn to the monument at dusk?

Team concludes: Because the lighting of the monument in the evening attracts the insects.

Resolution: Evaluate a different time to turn on monument lighting to prevent the attraction of insects.

This approach requires in-depth discussion and brainstorming; the team shares alternatives as a group and in a nonjudgmental fashion. It requires that participants classify, categorize, and prioritize the issues driving the problem. Brainstorming exercises help to establish patterns and relationships among the facts that will be analyzed in terms of the problem criteria.

Systematic problem-solving is a standardized approach toward facilitating a conversation and promoting deep understanding and critical thinking in order to find a subjective solution to a situation by defining a problem, conducting analysis, determining the cause of the problem, developing corrective actions, and monitoring results.

Define the Problem

This is a critical phase in which the problem-solving team outlines a problem statement for the organization, recognizing that there is a gap between what is and what should be occurring in the process. Developing a problem statement is a process that shapes the problem-solving from start to finish in an actionable way. It is an opportunity for the problem-solving team to establish a clear idea of exactly which problem they are trying to solve. It is imperative to avoid any assumption in the problem statement that may suggest a potential root cause. Avoid conjunctions such as *because, due to, since, for the reason that, then, subsequently, after,* and *afterward,* among others. These words may prevent the problem-solving team from focusing, making it hard for them to know what they are aiming for and trying to achieve.

The problem-solving team seeks to understand the needs and requirements of the individuals or the groups who will receive the good/service of the process and translate that information into measurable requirements—doing so provides the team with insight on how to solve a problem. It is critical that the problem statement clearly and realistically includes the resources available to work on the problem; a reasonable time frame must also be considered. Answering each of the following questions can help the problem-solving team to zero in on the specific issue:

1. What is the issue?
2. What impact does the issue have on the business or

customer?
3. Who does the problem affect?
4. Where does the issue occur?
5. When does the issue occur?
6. How many parts are involved?
7. When does it need to be fixed?
8. What are the boundaries of the problem?
9. Why is it important that we fix the problem?
10. What will happen when it is fixed?

The problem-solving team should avoid the following when defining a problem statement:

1. Addressing more than one problem
2. Making assumptions about problem causes
3. Assigning blame
4. Offering solutions

Having a good problem statement ensures that the problem-solving team fully understands the goal, keeps them on track, and helps the team to articulate what, when, the impact, and who is affected by the problem. As the problem-solving team advances through the problem-solving process, they will constantly refer to the problem statement to make sure they are moving in the right direction.

Conduct Analysis

Conducting analysis involves a range of analytic activities with the purpose of representing, communicating, and laying out information to understand the internal work of a process. A completed process flow diagram can be used as a baseline to identify and measure tasks within the process. How does the problem-solving team identify what to measure? Well, the team needs to identify which tasks have results that are measurable and inform current performance. By "measurable," I mean that the objective or the outcome of a task can be noticed or detected. For instance, this would include a task outcome that is defective, needs to be reworked, or utilizes completion count per hour. Therefore, if the outcome can't be observed, then the problem-solving team can't measure it. This is a very important step, because if the team doesn't know the result of the tasks or activities mapped, how can they recognize what is happening?

Measures provide the problem-solving team with objective and quantitative evidence of results. Remember that the intention is to measure results and not activities or activity milestones. Once measures are defined and implemented for more than three months (I suggest a minimum of three months' worth of data), then the problem-solving team has enough information for descriptive data and the application of data illustration tools, such as a histogram, pareto, scatter plot, and box plot, among others. These illustration tools will be covered later. Applying the right illustrative tool is critical to providing true comprehension of the process performance and identifying process deficiencies. Information gathered throughout the process analysis is used by the problem-solving team to bring about a flow of how the activities are taking place, from their beginning until they achieve the purpose of the process. To conduct process analysis, data gathering from a system or data collection are key steps to being successful at data analysis.

Data analysis deals with information, while interpretation is concerned with what happens in a process. In my opinion, data analysis is an art and a data analyst is an artist. Almost anyone can pull data from any computer system and dump it onto a spreadsheet to get the average of the data pulled, but is that data analysis? Is the data correct? Does the data make sense in terms of the problem to be solved? Probably not. Is retrieving such information easy or effective?

Data analysis is a systematic process of collecting data, data cleansing, describing data, and illustrating data to facilitate a decision-making process.

Collecting Data

Gathering raw data at the source is the initial step for collecting data once every question is clearly defined and the goals are properly set. The problem-solving team is accountable for deciding how to gather the data, or translating the problem defined into a model that can then be objectively analyzed. There are two main ways to gather data: either by direct observation and measurement, or by pulling standard data from a predetermined information system such as finance, accounting, human resources, inventory, procurement and acquisition, sales, marketing, material, or operation databases. Let's start reviewing the latter.

Collecting data from a determined electronic record system implies that the problem-solving team already knows what information to look for and where to find it. It means that there is an information technology system integrated with a process for data collection and reporting. For instance, in a health systems environment, it is well-known that an information technology system exists for hospital registration and admissions. The same is applicable to a manufacturing operation where the information technology infrastructure to fully support quality, inventory, and warehouse management is developed for incorporating this information into operational data flows. However, does the problem-solving team know the type of data they need?

It is important that the problem-solving team understand the types of data they are dealing with; they will then be able to identify data entry errors. The basic data types, such as categorical and continuous data, are critical to know since this information allows the problem-solving team to identify appropriate data analysis. Categorical and continuous data are divided into two subcategories, and the team must be able to identify whether categorical data is nominal or ordinal. Nominal data is a discrete unit that has no inherent ordering, such as countries, cities, gender, race, ethnicity, or language. On the other hand, ordinal data is a discrete unit in which value describes the numerical position of an object, such as first, second, and third.

Continuous data is measured as finely as possible and can include fractions and decimals—for instance, distance, time, money, and temperature. The two subgroups of continuous data are interval and range. Intervals are built upon an ordinal scale with units of the same size. For example, the difference between 15° and 20° is the same as 45° and 50°. An important distinction of the interval scale is that it is limited by lack of an absolute zero value. For example, living human bodies cannot have zero gallons of blood. Moreover, the least volume of blood in an adult human body is 1.5 gallons. On the other hand, ratio data includes absolute zero along with all the properties of interval scales. Time is an example of ratio, since individuals can start measuring time at zero.

Even though this data type explanation seems very elemental, individuals must ensure understanding on the distinction between categorical and continuous data. It is important to identify the type of data in a variable before deciding the statistical methods and data illustration to use, because methods are designed to work with certain types of data. The problem-solving team needs to avoid producing a wrong analysis.

Gathering data by direct observation of a system in operation requires following specific work measurement methods: work sampling and time and motion study. Both methods will be introduced followed by health-care case studies for a better understanding of their applications and what conclusions may be obtained following application.

Work Sampling

Work sampling is a technique that helps determine the length of time it takes to complete a job. This technique collects data at intervals of time by observing an individual in action at the point in time selected for the observation. For example, data might be collected by determining what an individual is doing every fifteen minutes. The work-sampling approach is used most frequently when individuals are in a circumscribed area, such as clinical units in a hospital, a manufacturing plant floor, and office operations. The following example is a walk-through of the application of the work-sampling technique.

Registered nurses (RNs) at seven inpatient clinical units were subject to a work-sampling study to have a clear vision of how nurses use their time. The purpose is to determine the distribution of activities performed by nurses and to determine value and nonvalue-added tasks.

The work sampling was scheduled to conduct random observations for two weeks. The observation time consisted of two-hour blocks twice per unit (two blocks per unit) or a total of fourteen blocks of two hours for a total of twenty-eight hours.

The observer was tasked to record work activities performed by four different RNs every two minutes until the two-hour blocks were completed. Therefore, thirty data points were expected per hour block or sixty data points per two-hour blocks. The following equation summarizes the total data points observed during the work-sampling exercise resulting in 3,360 data points observed.

$$(2-hour\,block)\left(30\frac{data\,points}{hour\,block}\right)\left(2\frac{blocks}{unit}\right)\left(4\frac{nurses\,observed}{block}\right)(7\,units) =$$

$$(7\,units) = 3360\,data\,points\,observed$$

Table 1 shows a sample of the work sampling for nurses at randomly selected times and types of activities that are observed at that instance.

The x-axis displays the time (in minutes) scheduled for observations. Every two minutes, a mental snapshot was taken of where the surrounding nurses were at each point in time. The total number for each activity witnessed was documented underneath the corresponding time. The left column shows the task categories of generalized activities performed by the nurses. For example, "Patient care" refers to anything involving

Table 1: Observation record form designed for study of nurses' tasks

Task \ Time (min)	2	4	6	8	10	12	14	16	18	20	22	24	26	28	30
Patient care	①	②	③	③	④	③	④	⑤	③	③	⑤	④	⑦	③	⑤
Computer	②	①	②	②	①	①	②	②	②	④	④	④	④	④	①
Communication	③	①		①	①			②	①		①	②	①	③	②
Search for supplies			②	①	①	①	②	①	②	①			③	③	①
Check in															
Documentation	①	①	①				①	①	①						①
Medicine															
Equipment setup							①	①	①			②			
Transportation							①	①	①	①			①		
Handoff													①	①	①
Personal										①					
Washing after patient care										①					
Rounding													①		
Admission															
Miscellaneous															
Discharge															
Escalation															
Cleaning															
Huddle															

The numbers in the matrix represent number of random nurses observed at a specific time.

treatment or responding to a patient's needs, including scheduled interventions, or in response to a call bell. The complete description for the tasks can be found in Table 2.

Data collected was analyzed by producing a treemap chart, Figure 6, where observations were categorized by the tasks performed by nurses. Of the 3,360 observations made, 1,134 were of patient care, 492 were of computers, 319 were searching for supplies, 293 were of communication, 219 for rounding, 119 for check-in, and 95 for huddles, among others.

The work-sampling data of all tasks observed is categorized into one of three topics: bedside interventions, bedside

Table 2: Brief description of each task included in the observation record form

Tasks	Description
Patient care	Treatment, responding to bed/call alarms, rapid response
Computer	Charting, patient information, or any activity on the computer
Communication	Interaction between nurses and physicians, incoming/outgoing calls
Searching for supplies	In supply room, equipment room, med room, hallway, or vacant rooms looking for items
Check in	Quick visit with the patient to see how they are
Documentation	Any written documenting
Medicine	Giving medication to the patient
Equipment setup	Setting up workstation on wheels, scale
Transportation	RNs helping transport admit/discharge patients
Handoff	Shift change, handoff to physicians
Personal	Lunch, bathroom breaks
Washing after patient care	Washing hands at open sink station after patient care
Rounding	Purposeful rounding on patients
Admission	New patient admission, patient coming back from different unit
Miscellaneous	Explaining to observer, walking in hall, waiting, or any new observations
Discharge	Preparing patient for discharge or discharging a patient
Escalation	Asking charge nurse or RN available for assistance in tasks unable to complete
Cleaning	Preparing for admission or cleaning rooms
Huddle	Morning, mid-shift, and safety huddles

support, or other. These categories show the amount of time directly spent with a patient, time spent away from the patient, focused on supporting those bedside intervention actions, and all other activities. The breakdown of the categories can be seen in a pie chart, Figure 7, which is a circular graph proportionally divided to the magnitudes of the observations represented in percentage. Bucketing the tasks gives the ability to see the most common activity within each of the categories as shown in the Bedside Intervention Tasks bar graph.

Organizing the data by task per activity easily depicts how the nurses spend their time with patients (see Figure 8). Forty-nine percent of the work documented was performed at the

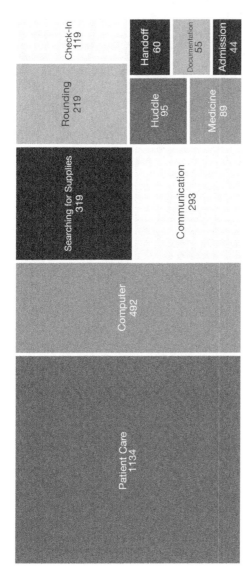

Figure 6: Number of observations by task

Top 11 task outcomes in the work sampling

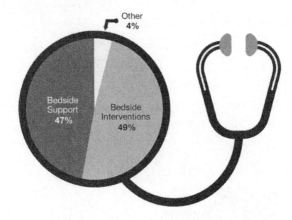

Figure 7: Nurse tasks by category

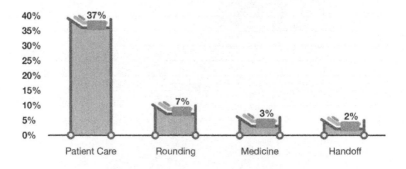

Figure 8: Percent of observations per Bedside Intervention Tasks

bedside caring for the patient; 37% of the time observed, the RNs were treating patients or rapidly responding to call bells/ bed alarms.

Objectively, 51% of the activities were done outside of the patient rooms. Forty-seven percent of the 51% was spent supporting those bedside processes and 4% was spent on other tasks. The Bedside Support Activities bar graph, Figure 9, illustrates that bedside support activities are concentrated on executing the patient plan of care. Seventeen percent of the bedside support activities were related to nurses on the computer. Working on the computer includes charting patient progress, looking up patient information, paging physicians, or searching the Internet. By the same token, 10% of the time, nurses were busy searching for supplies.

The remaining 4% is devoted to all other processes nurses go through during their shifts. Please refer to the Other Activities bar graph for details in Figure 10. Bedside interventions, bedside support activities, and other activities do not guarantee those processes are value added or wasted. The largest contribution to nonvalue-added activities is the 4% under Other Activities. This captured nurses walking in the hallway to a patient room, waiting for orders, or waiting for a doctor to call regarding the plan of care.

The work-sampling study was initiated to determine the proportion of time allocated to bedside patient care activities and other nursing activities in order to identify nonvalue-added activities and to look for effective ways of staffing. Nurses' efficiencies in performing required tasks can significantly improve by addressing the opportunities defined here. It has been demonstrated that nurses spend more time treating patients and responding to patients' needs; however, approximately the same amount of time is spent by the nurses on patient acuity support activities. A further study is recommended to analyze opportunities for improvement related to the flow of information and supplies required for patient acuity.

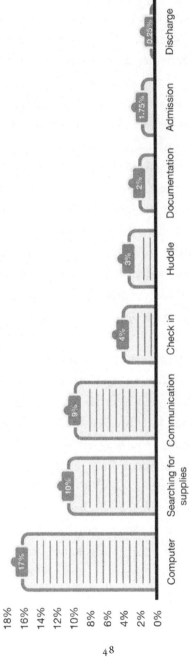

Figure 9: Percent of observations per Bedside Support Tasks

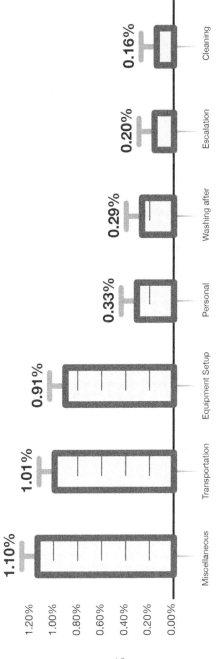

Figure 10: Percent of observations per Other Tasks

Time and Motion Study

The time and motion study is a method of analyzing the time required by a qualified individual to complete a specific task by timing each job element within the process to determine which activities don't add value to a process. Through the time and motion study, it is possible to calculate a process capacity to improve efficiency and productivity. During this process, it is important to define the task subject to this measurement as to elements; then the time gathered for each element is summed up to get the total time after discounting personal time (breaks, supervisor instructions, meetings), delays that are not under the control of the individual performing the task, and loss of production due to fatigue.

To be successful at this method, it is important to take more than one work sample. The problem-solving team needs to account for many work samples on different days and in different circumstances. Once they have various work samples, the team will have a better understanding and sense of reality of the task, and will be more adequately prepared to observe the challenges that individuals constantly face when completing that task.

The time and measurement study, also known as a stopwatch time study, is an old technique developed by Frederick W. Taylor before the turn of the twentieth century. It is a very technical method, so I suggest researching and studying the mechanics of how to properly conduct a stopwatch time study.

Next, we will learn how the outcome of a stopwatch time study was applied. The purpose of this study was to understand and identify opportunities to increase utilization of seven radiology oncology examination rooms accommodating patients' appointments. In order to gather enough data, observations took place over approximately two weeks and were scheduled from 7:30 a.m. to 3:00 p.m. An observer was stationed in the unit to capture the task each staff conducted while patients were called back from the main waiting room in the lobby. There were three types of appointments observed: (1) consultation (new/returning), (2) follow-up, and (3) on-site treatment care (OTC). These appointment types are the tasks assessed.

Over two hundred observations were conducted to accurately measure the average process time associated with each activity to either OTC, consult, or follow up with patients. Direct observations allowed validation of the sequence of elements defined for each task.

The mean and standard deviation of such times for all observations are shown in Table 3. The results show the amount of waiting that occurred within the process flow.

The analysis consisted of observing 203 patients as they entered the unit and were discharged. The results of the average

Table 3: Means and standard deviations of OTC, consult, or follow-up activities observed in seven radiology oncology examination rooms

Suppliers	Mean (Min)	Std (Min)
Patient preparation by RN before MD consultation	6.5	1.88
Waiting for doctor	14.0	2.2
Consultation/Follow-Up	17	4.8

Table 4: Average percentage of room vacancy for the radiology oncology examination rooms

Room 1	Room 2	Room 3	Room 4	Room 5	Room 6	Room 7
60%	58%	43%	52%	86%	77%	93%

percentages of room vacancy (during the hours of observation) are as follows:

The Average Room Vacancies by Observation Days bar chart shows all seven examination rooms for two weeks.

The data demonstrates that all rooms are currently underutilized, indicating that no more rooms are required.

The time spent in the room depends on the type of diagnostic or treatment procedures. Therefore, the time spent by the patients in the examination rooms was compared for each appointment type: consultation, follow-up, and OTC. Notice that Figure 12 shows the breakdown of patients' time spent in the exam room per appointment type. The breakdown is in minutes, consisting of patients' waiting time alone in the exam room, nurse present in the room with the patient, and the time spent by the physician in the room with the patient.

The results of the time and measurement study for the 203 patients observed show that all three appointment types average 40% of the observed time when physicians spend time with patients in the exam rooms (18 minutes on average). Similarly, 28% of the time is attributed to nurses in the exam room with patients. However, a patient spends between 31% and 33% of the time, approximately, waiting for either a nurse or physician to join them in the exam room. These percentages

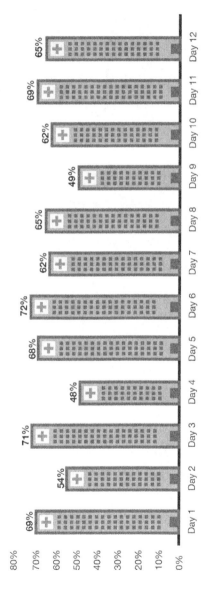

Figure 11: Radiology oncology examination rooms vacancy rate

Average percentage of all seven radiology oncology examination rooms available by observation days

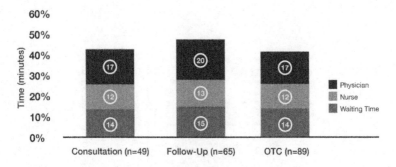

Figure 12: Average cycle time by service offered
Patients' average time spent with physicians, nurses, or waiting alone once in the radiology oncology examination rooms.

represent between 14 and 15 minutes of waiting time. Waiting time doesn't add value to any process. So, 33% of the process attributed to waiting time is a symptom that something is going wrong. We must take a closer look to find out what exactly is causing such a lengthy waiting time in the exam room.

From this analysis, some recommendations can be made for improvement and further analysis.

1. Create a standard schedule of work. There should be a "standard work" meeting, which would include the staff who actually perform the task (nurses or front desk), management, physicians, and support from a strategic process improvement representative. Standardizing the scheduling process will hopefully minimize the number of add-on patients or surprise appointments for those very busy days. It will also prevent in-patients

from being transported down to the unit and stationed in the hallway as opposed to the designated bay.

2. Review all protocols and identify how multidisciplinary collaboration can improve.

3. Further assess nurses' and physicians' activities while outside the exam room.

4. Analyze patient schedule block time and how patients' late arrivals and no-shows affect the radiology oncology appointment process.

Data Cleansing

At this point, the problem-solving team is ready to take a closer look at the data gathered or collected at all the necessary sources. First, review the data set by identifying the variables and observations contained in it. Usually, a data set is organized in templates consisting of columns (vertically) and rows (horizontally) where each column is a variable and each row contains observations for each variable. Second, ensure that all observations for each variable are formatted as desired (i.e., %, #, $, date, or text) and modify or eliminate the data that is incorrect. Keep in mind that data is not always good data and sometimes is unnecessary, unfinished, or unrelated. Third, clean the data by eliminating duplicates, correcting empty fields or cells as needed, and fixing syntax errors. However, this is not a process for deleting information to fit new data. Correcting anomalous information before analyzing data is an extremely important step in generating accurate results and avoiding skewed analysis.

A different approach can be taken to clean up inconsistent data for different problem contexts. Data cleansing can be easily done in MS Excel and other open-source tools. Problem-solving teams must keep in mind that data cleansing is all about creating data sets that are standardized and uniform in an effort to maximize accuracy without necessarily deleting information. Addressing the following ten questions can help the team through the data cleansing process.

1. Does the problem-solving team need to back up the data set?
2. Is the data categorical, continuous, or both?
3. Do character variables and date values have valid values?
4. Are numeric variables within range?
5. Are the values recorded in the same unit value? (i.e., 90% vs. 0.90)
6. Are there null or missing values?
7. Are there duplicate values?
8. Is there more than one abbreviation for the same value?
9. Are there spelling mistakes?
10. Is there any arithmetic or logical function applied to calculate data?

Checking off these questions can help the problem-solving team manage the data cleansing process. While this process can be overwhelming, other processes might be straightforward. The key in this process is for the team to have a solid understanding of the context in the data, as well as the problems they are trying to solve.

Describing Data

Dealing with data can be an overwhelming exercise, especially if we are just looking for a single number that can yield information. However, applying descriptive statistics helps with the analysis process, giving one the opportunity to understand, summarize, and describe a data set. Even so, applying this process does not mean that we can reach conclusions regarding the problem under consideration. Descriptive statistics simply describe the data in consideration, not the problem.

Individuals are surrounded by statistics on a daily basis. For instance, when hearing or reading in the morning that the chance of rain is 75%, people make a decision about how to dress for the day and may grab an umbrella before leaving home. This kind of forecast information is based on statistical analysis as well as how long it will take to get to your final destination when relying on information given by smart devices. At the same time, individuals hear from the news media when stock prices have risen or fallen. People can observe this information in action using historical data. The stock prices typically follow a normal distribution in which most investment returns fall within one standard deviation of the mean.

These are some examples of how everybody has been using statistical verbiage daily, while the news media uses statistics constantly to demonstrate changes in trends. Descriptive statistics are very important because they help present raw data that would be hard to visualize. Nevertheless, how to properly describe data through statistics and graphs is an important subject in data analysis.

Let's introduce some basic statistical concepts. Descriptive statistics involves summarizing data in a way that it is easy to understand. When collecting data on a single variable, descriptive statistics helps make sense about the single variable by describing the central distribution or tendency of the data collected. Central distribution plays an important role in understanding the location that represents the typical value or the value that is expected of the variable under consideration. *Central tendency* is that value that describes a data set by identifying its central position. Measures of central tendency represent this idea with a value. The central tendency is used because it summarizes the data set down to one representative value. There are three familiar measures (averages) for describing central tendency: mean, median, and mode. These three types of measures are averages. The term "average" refers to the middle point. For this reason, we frequently use the term *average* in all sorts of contexts. For instance, we might say, "I had an average score," meaning that the score is neither particularly good nor bad; it is about normal. The most widely used method of calculating an average is the mean, also known as the arithmetic mean.

The mean is simply the sum (Σ) of all data values (x_i) divided by the total numbers (N) included in the data set. This value, the mean, looks at the center of the data set. The formula below shows how to calculate the mean.

$$\mu = \frac{1}{N} \sum_{i=1}^{N} x_i$$

Where

μ = Mean

N = Total number of counts in the data set

$\sum$ = Summation. Add numbers up to whatever comes after it

x_i = Value of each individual item in the list of numbers being averaged

i = The subscript notation to specify an index for the first, second, and third value, and so forth

The median is the middle number of the data set when the numbers are ordered from greatest to least in value. In other words, to find the median, it is necessary to have all values (expenses) in the data set sorted in ascending order and then divide the data into two equal parts. The number that is halfway into the set is the median. If there is an even number of values in the data set, then we take the mean of the two middlemost values to find the median.

There is the mode, in which the values from a data set are sorted in ascending order and then counted, revealing the value that shows up the most. The mean or the median is usually a much more useful measure of central tendency than the mode.

Although central tendency gives information about the center of the distribution in the data set, it does not accurately represent every value in the distribution. For instance, values can be higher or lower than the mean. For this reason, it is highly recommended that the problem-solving team understands the variability of the distribution. Variability of the distribution refers to the dispersion of values in the data set.

When reviewing values in the data set, finding out the difference between the largest value and the smallest value gives the range. The range provides information on how spread apart the values in the data set are. Another way to get information about variability of the distribution is by calculating the standard deviation.

Standard deviation is determined by calculating the distance from each value to the mean, then squaring every distance calculated to find the mean of those squared distances. The greater the number calculated as the standard deviation, the more spread out the data distribution. Conversely, a standard deviation close to zero indicates that the data values tend to be close to the mean. Please refer to the formula below.

$$\sigma = \sqrt{\frac{\sum \left(x_i - \mu\right)^2}{N}}$$

Where
σ = population standard deviation
μ = population mean
N = count of numbers in the population
x_i = value of each number in the population

Forgotten monthly expenses is an example for data description. Forgetting to include necessary expenses in a personal monthly budget can be a common error. We must admit that there are times we forget to budget for expenses such as privately hired transportation, birthday presents, car repair and registration, holidays, haircuts, etc. This example shows descriptive statistics of forgotten monthly expenses for three months (see Table 5).

Illustrating Data

Data illustration and data storytelling are the hottest topics in business intelligence these days. Data illustration, also known as data visualization, is used to understand behavioral patterns of any kind. I tend to appreciate easily distinguishable lines, bars, shapes, size, and colors, especially if these are graphically displayed in a way that is understandable and relatable.

Many stories can be told through their data points; visualization displays information about relationships that are already understood. It is simple to identify the relationships between the variables to support the narrative. However, it must be understood that data illustration for presentation is

Table 5: Forgotten monthly expenses in US dollars

Expenses ($)								
Month 1			**Month 2**			**Month 3**		
11	69	33	28	20	35	18	38	21
8	26	35	18	6	26	38	8	14
28	22	10	21	20	23	37	13	58
10	80	6	17	25	18	16	12	35
6	48	49	24	18	29	62	17	38
27	12	24	21	22	55	20	24	9
6	19	21	15	5	16	17	28	30
20	6	37	5	14	31	5	28	24
25	50	37	38	11	62	12	18	22
14	32	25	22	40	10	32	26	38
Total		796	Total		695	Total		758
Mean		27	Mean		23	Mean		25
Median		25	Median		21	Median		23
Mode		6	Mode		18	Mode		38
Std		18.5	Std		13.0	Std		13.6

Mean	$25.00
Median	$22.00
Mode	$18.00
Standard Deviation	$15.04

not the same as data illustration for analysis. The data illustration gives information of *what* story you desire to tell, while the narrative provides answers to *why*. The narrative considers all assumptions made since it is expected that the data is known in its context. Think about it: this gives your audience something else to look at that is easy to understand. They can then follow the story you desire to tell.

There are graphical images such as charts, graphs, or maps that can be developed to best describe a content while depicting the big picture. The options are almost endless. Let's list some examples in Table 6.

Plots or charts help one to quickly see how values are related to each other. Histograms, box plots, and scatter plots are ways of looking at many related values without looking at bunches of numbers. For instance, if the problem-solving team is interested in demonstrating the data set distribution or the relationship between two variables or more, they must rely on a specific type of graph. Basically, a bar chart is useful for

Table 6: Types of data visualization

Visual Type	Description
Infographics	A form of an attractive visual graphic of any kind (charts, graphs, icons, and text) that presents information to capture audience attention and enhance comprehension.
GIFs	Graphics interchange formats are animated images, but not videos, with the purpose to communicate emotion, reactions, and ideas.
Treemap	Displays data information hierarchically representing quantity in nested rectangles; the larger the data point, the bigger the rectangle.
Geographical graph	Plots data measures corresponding to a geographical location; for instance, gross domestic product per country.
Heat map	Displays data using colors in two dimensions (i.e., black and white) representing the magnitude of data information by variating the density of the color spectrum.
Bar graph	A chart that depicts data information by any given category using either horizontal or vertical bars.
Line graph	A chart that plots the data information behavior over time by connecting data points with straight lines.
Pie chart	A chart that shows data information proportional to the fraction by categories that make up the whole.

comparing values with few categories, the line or trend graph compares behaviors over time, and the scatter plot shows relationships between two continuous variables. Moreover, the histogram is used to depict the distribution of the data set, even though that aspect could also be shown through scatter plots. Pie charts are beneficial to show the composition of data. Therefore, the type of data illustration depends upon the variables being analyzed.

Histogram

A histogram is an important statistical tool for displaying frequency distribution data in a bar chart. What does this mean? A data set is distributed and grouped into bins to show how many data points are counted (frequency) against each bin. A bin is a data subset used when splitting the data into intervals. These bins represent a subclassification of the data. Each bin is represented by a bar that indicates the relative frequencies of values in the data set. In other words, data point totals fall into specific bins. The purpose of a histogram is to display how your data is spread out.

How to Build a Histogram

Identify the minimum and maximum data value in the data set. Then, subtract these two values to compute the range. Once the data range is determined, find the number of bins by a number between five and 20. There is no rule that specifies a number by which to divide the range; however, in practice, use five for small sets of data and 20 for larger sets. Once the number of

Table 7: Restaurant consumption expenses for three months in US dollars

Month 1			Month 2			Month 3		
$11	$69	$33	$28	$20	$35	$18	$38	$21
$8	$26	$35	$18	$6	$26	$38	$8	$14
$28	$22	$10	$21	$20	$23	$37	$13	$58
$10	$80	$6	$17	$25	$18	$16	$12	$35
$6	$48	$49	$24	$18	$29	$62	$17	$38
$27	$12	$24	$21	$22	$55	$20	$24	$9
$6	$19	$21	$15	$5	$16	$17	$28	$30
$20	$6	$37	$5	$14	$31	$5	$28	$24
$25	$50	$37	$38	$11	$62	$12	$18	$22
$14	$32	$25	$22	$40	$10	$32	$26	$38

bins is calculated, determine a bin range that will include the lowest data value. Subsequently, use the bin range to build subsequent bins until reaching the bin with the highest data value. Then count the number of occurrences of the values in the data set that are contained within that bin.

Let's apply the histogram analysis to an example that people can relate to: forgotten monthly expenses. It is assumed that restaurants are the largest forgotten monthly expense, with an average total of $750. Table 7 details each restaurant consumption for the last three months. Each value included in the table is rounded to the nearest tenth. The maximum value is $80, and the minimum value is $5. When subtracting both values, we find the range of 75. It is determined that the data set is considered a small data set, so the range is divided by five to set the width of the bins. In Figure 13 the distribution graph shows that five bins (5–20,

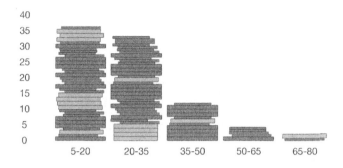

40
35
30
25
20
15
10
5
0

5-20   20-35   35-50   50-65   65-80

Figure 13: Distribution of forgotten monthly expenses
Bell curve is skewed to the right or positively skewed, meaning
that the arithmetic mean is to the right of the median value.

20–35, 35–50, 50–65, 65–80) are set, and the frequency
for each bin is applied.

For instance, there are 33 values within the data set that fall
between 20 and 35. Now that the histogram is built, what do
we get out of it?

Notice that the visualization shows information as it exists,
assuming a bell-curve shape. The bell-curve shape is a common
characteristic to analyze, gives information that will help show
where to look, and offers some insights into what the data set
says. A curve shape could be skewed to the right, looking like
an uneven mound with a tail going off to the right, but like a
bell-curve shape. The same applies if the curve is skewed to
the left. For instance, a distribution of analyses of the forgotten
monthly expenses is skewed because the expense data shows
much less data greater than $35 per meal.

Another way to organize and analyze the same data set is
by building categories or labels as shown in Figure 14.

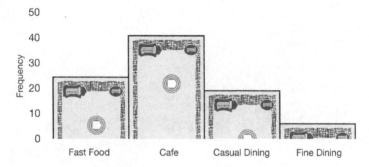

Figure 14: Histogram of type of restaurants

This visualization shows four bins: fast food, café, casual dining, and fine dining. This approach considers fast-food with an expense range from $0 to $15, cafe ($15-$30), casual dining ($30-$50), and fine dining ($50-$80). This is what the restaurant expense dispersion looks like, skewed off to the left: very few expenses are made to fine and casual dining, while most expenses are attributed to the café. Even though the shapes and types of data are skewed to the left, the central tendency can be determined. That's the area in the distribution where the bulk of the expenses tend to occur.

The mean of the restaurant expense is $25. Consider the middle of the data set: the median is $22. Since the central tendency falls in the café range, we should reduce the frequency of visits to this type of restaurant (remember that the goal is to cut forgotten monthly expenses). Emphasis in this range may help to push the curve off to the right. This thought leads one to look at the dispersion of the histogram. "Dispersion" refers to the variability in the expenses and allows us to identify how spread out the expenses are. It measures how much the expenses vary from the central tendency. It seems that the dispersion of the expenses is centrally located around the mean $25, although there are some expenses a little farther from the $25, such as those expenses in the Fine Dining bin.

The histogram allows us to identify where opportunities for improvement reside, therefore helping the problem-solving team to focus on those areas. Also, it gives team guidance for making decisions based on the information graphed.

Box and Whiskers Plot

The box and whiskers plot, also known as the box plot, is a graphical description used to understand how quantitative data is distributed. It displays the minimum, first quartile, median, third quartile, and maximum, suggesting the shape of the distribution of the data set, its central value, and its variability. The problem-solving team can use this plot illustration while dealing with a large data set, or while comparing multiple data sets. It is very useful for visualizing whether the spread of the data is skewed and whether there are potential outliers in the data set. In a box plot, there are six components to look after: minimum value, whiskers, quartiles and the interquartile range, median, maximum value, and outliers.

As previously discussed, the median gives a measure of the center (see Figure 15). There are two quartiles: a lower quartile (Q1) and an upper quartile (Q3). This makes Q2 the median. The lower quartile is the 25th percentile, meaning that is the lower extreme that contains the first 25% of all data (0-25%). Q2 is the 50th percentile, or the area in the box with the second 25% of all data (25-50%). The upper quartile is the 75th percentile of the data showing the area in the box

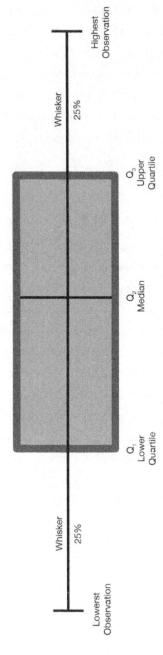

Figure 15: Box and whisker plot
Approximately 25% of a data set is contained in each section of the box and whisker plot.

with the third 25% of all data (50-75%). Finally, the fourth quartile (Q4) is the upper extreme that contains from 75% to 100% of the data.

Therefore, the distance between Q1 and Q3 gives information about how spread out the middle 50% of the data is. This illustrates the box that is the interquartile range. Including the minimum and maximum values will give the overall range for the data set. Five numbers give us a box plot illustration.

It is important to understand that the box plot gives a quick statistical summary of how a data set is distributed. Also, when there are outliers, the lower and upper lines outside the box have different meanings, and when there are not outliers, the lowest and the highest observations are the minimum and maximum values, respectively.

Scatter Plot

The scatter plot is best used when illustrating the relationship between paired data and the scheme pattern of a data set. Usually, the plot follows a linear pattern when plotting each data point individually, using values in both the y-axis and x-axis. Clearly, this can help you understand how one variable affects another. The outcome of the scatter plot drives the analysis mainly for correlation, or the relationship between two variables. Also, studying the plot helps to identify data outliers.

There is positive correlation if y-axis values increase as x-axis values also increase in the scatter plot. However, a negative correlation occurs when the y-axis values tend to decrease as the x-axis values increase. If the scatter plot outcome shows no linear pattern, then there is no correlation in the paired data.

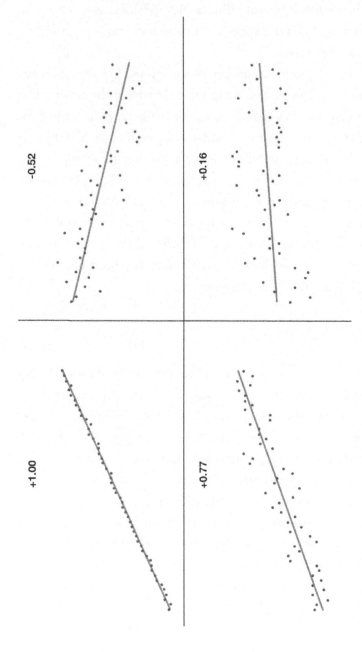

Figure 16: Scatter plot illustrations with correlations of +1.00, -0.52, +0.77, and +0.16

In addition, a mathematical algorithm can be used to calculate the correlation coefficient and thereby identify the correlation.

The correlation coefficient is a measure usually represented by the letter r, which explains the strength and direction of a linear relationship between two variables. The measured values are always between $+1$ and -1. When the correlation coefficient is exactly -1 or 1, it means it is perfectly correlated, while $r = 0$ means no correlation.

How can the problem-solving team interpret this correlation coefficient r? After calculating the correlation coefficient and graphing the scatter plot outcome, the problem-solving team can analyze how much randomness there is between the y-axis and x-axis variables, as well as how one variable linearly affects the other variable. For instance, observe two random variables at the same time, such as *likes* in social media and profit. If this variable relationship seems to correlate in a somewhat positive direction, it might have a value of 0.74, whereas a weak negative correlation might have the value -0.32. Therefore, the closer the correlation coefficient is to zero, the weaker the correlation.

It is very important that the problem-solving team does not confuse correlation with causation, even though correlation can sometimes be a coincidence. Causation implies that, for example, receiving *likes* in social media causes profit increase, or vice versa. Causation is saying that *likes* in social media and profit have a cause-and-effect relationship with one another. Causation or causality means that the existence of one variable causes the other variable to manifest, while this is not the case in correlation analysis. Remember—using the scatter plot the proper way to illustrate the relationship of two continuous variables with a correlation is just a mechanism to determine the extent to which two variables resemble one another.

Pareto Analysis

This is a statistical approach that uses data to recognize how many predefined causal factors have occurred in any business process or system. It is premised on the classic 80/20 rule, which presumes that 80% of your problems are due to 20% of the causes. This outcome may give the problem-solving team information about which causes to address first. The team will observe the problems and determine their frequency of occurrence. This exercise will provide information to prioritize, ensuring that the team is spending time where their efforts will have the most positive impact.

For instance, let's say that you want to analyze forgotten monthly expenses. Pareto analysis is a useful tool to help address financial problems, or a common problem with multiple financial commitments. This technique can be used to find a monthly expense pattern that can generate the greatest impact while taking into account the most significant monthly financial commitments.

Now you are ready to collect some information to conduct the analysis. Decide what expenses will be considered for the analysis. Then determine the occurrence or frequency of the expenses (biweekly, monthly, quarterly, annually). Next, build up a table with the data and information collected. Sort the data by the amount of money committed as the monthly expense in descending order (see Table 8). The purpose of sorting the data in descending order is to show where most of

Table 8: Forgotten monthly expense amounts arranged in descending order

Cumulative percent of total is calculated to build a Pareto diagram

Forgotten Monthly Expenses	Amount	Percentage	Cumulative %
Restaurants	$750	29.2%	29.2%
Entertainment	$690	26.8%	56.0%
Online shopping	$610	23.7%	79.8%
Public transportation	$190	7.4%	87.2%
Clothing	$120	4.7%	91.8%
Gifts	$80	3.1%	94.9%
Credit card interest	$55	2.1%	97.1%
Subscription	$40	1.6%	98.6%
Laundry	$35	1.4%	100.0%
Total	$2,570	100%	

the monthly expenses occur. Then find the monthly total of expenses being considered and find the percentage that each expense represents of the total amount per month. Now it is easy to calculate the cumulative percentage of each expense. This process can help you focus on the majority of expenses.

Once this table is built up, a vertical bar graph should be developed (see Figure 17). Notice that since the data was sorted in descending order, the bar chart is also organized from tallest to smallest. The chart's y-axis should represent the number of dollars spent, while the secondary axis (y-axis at the right) should represent the cumulative percentage calculated for each expense.

What are the monthly commitments that represent approximately 20% of the forgotten monthly expenses? From the chart, you can clearly determine that restaurants, entertainment, and online shopping together make up 79.8%. These are the expenses that you should focus on reducing. Pareto analysis

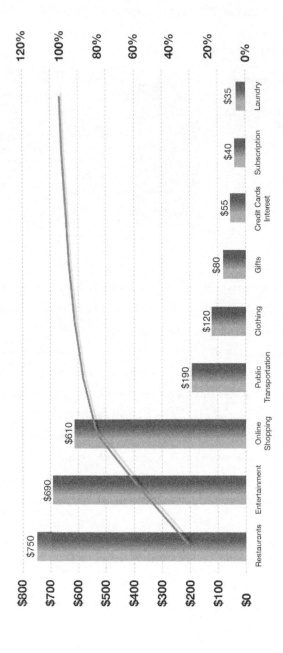

Figure 17: Pareto Diagram for forgotten monthly expenses

is a very useful tool for the problem-solving team to figure out problems in a workflow process.

Determining the Cause of the Problem

Root cause analysis (RCA) is a structured team process led by a problem-solver facilitator to identify causes and find out what happened and why it happened in order to develop corrective actions. RCA is usually implemented to address an event that resulted in an undesired outcome. The RCA process provides the team with a way to identify breakdowns in processes or systems that contributed to undesired events, and helps them understand how to prevent those events in the future.

What's causing our problems? Where should we start looking for solutions? These are some of the questions to which a problem-solving team would like answers. There are tools and methods that people refer to as RCA. The Five Whys analysis and the cause-and-effect diagram are the two most common methods for identifying possible causes that need to be addressed to prevent the problem from recurring.

Five Whys Analysis

This technique is a brainstorming method and the most simplistic RCA process. It involves repeatedly asking *why* at least five times or until you get to the root cause of the problem. By asking the question "Why?" five or more times, the team can delve deeper into the problem and find that the answers to the questions are interrelated. However, the Five Whys analysis method is inappropriate for any complicated event. This RCA technique is quite useful for minor problems that require nothing more than a basic discussion of an event.

Now, the question is, how do you drive a Five Whys conversation? The facilitator conducting the Five Whys exercise must begin by identifying the process stakeholders who are directly involved and those who are impacted by the process in question. Then, the facilitator provides a complete description of the problem to start a dialogue in which a common understanding of the problem is reached.

Each person participates in a brainstorming session conducted by the facilitator to identify all potential causes participants can think of that are major contributors to a problem. In my experience, this exercise works best when the facilitator allows participants to quietly write down, on a sticky note, one cause at a time without sharing their initial thoughts with the rest of the group. Typically, by having an open conversation at the beginning of the exercise, participants tend to have a discussion generating potential solutions rather than identifying causes. The rationale is to provide an environment where everybody thinks independently, has equal participation, and feels they contribute throughout the problem-solving process. This avoids extroverts leading the conversation, fixing ideas, and limiting passive individuals from sharing their thoughts, and it allows the exercise to capture diversified causes. Fixation on ideas is negative to this kind of exercise because it blocks out the opportunity to consider all potential causes that participants can think of based on their experience facing the problem. If all ideas are written down, they will always be available for the team to consider.

Once all potential causes are written down and posted, the facilitator and the group proceed to classify the causes into the following five groups, although the team can have as many groups as they feel are necessary: (1) method, (2) equipment, (3) supplies, (4) people, (5) information technology. The advantage of classifying the potential causes is to identify what process components have been affected the most by counting the number of causes under each. Given this information, the group can triangulate causes across groups, prioritize what group and which causes they would like to tackle first. These prioritizations must take into account the level of effort and the impact that the potential cause has on the process. Finally, a deep-dive conversation must happen; the team should analyze what is causing the recurrence of the issue under consideration.

The facilitator conducting the Five Whys exercise must consider that reaching the real root cause is when the team identifies areas that will impact a system or a process. The facilitator should not validate the team when they identify vague areas, such as lack of training, lack of time, or lack of resources/staff. These are just symptoms that can be considered indications of a larger problem. Conducting a RCA is a very thorough exercise that requires experience to seek out details and engage with the team to reveal causes that others may overlook.

Cause-and-Effect Diagram

A cause-and-effect diagram, also known as the fishbone diagram, is a well-known approach in conducting RCA. This tool was developed by Kaoru Ishikawa, a professor from the University of Tokyo, in the summer of 1943. It helps in brainstorming to identify possible causes of a problem, sorting causes of variations into useful categories, and organizing the mutual relationships between them. Also, it is a more structured approach than some other tools available for brainstorming, namely the Five Whys analysis. Notice that the cause-and-effect diagram identifies issues that cause our problems, versus a Pareto diagram, which prioritizes potential causes and puts those together in a vertical bar chart. The fishbone diagram is a visualization tool to group causes into different subcategories. These categories in their origins are the four M's: methods, materials, machines, manpower.

Look deeper into these four categories. Why only four? This tool was developed under a manufacturing environment where causes of a problem generally consist of the process designed to produce or manufacture a product (methods), the raw material and components assembled (materials), the equipment utilized throughout the production process (machines), and the people and stakeholders involved in the process (manpower). Causes here allow the problem-solving team to go deeper, all possible causes are listed, and solutions are encouraged without confining thinking. Causes are drawn primarily to illustrate the various causes of a problem by sorting out and relating the causes, provoking a deep-dive conversation to help identify the root cause.

Let's talk about the previous problem of forgotten monthly expenses. What about restaurants? Visiting restaurants on a monthly basis is fine, but what kind of restaurants? Expensive or moderately priced restaurants, fast-food restaurants or food trucks? How frequently do I visit these restaurants? How many people do I treat when I visit the restaurants? Do I visit the restaurant for the three meals of the day? So, keep asking these kinds of questions until finally you get to the root cause. The idea of the fishbone diagram is to show causes so actions can be taken.

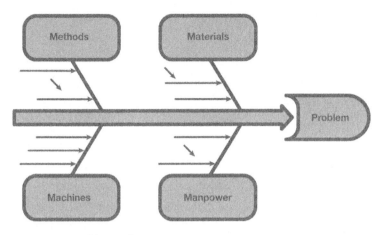

Figure 18: Fishbone diagram

The following general steps give some guidance on how to build a cause-and-effect diagram:

1. Describe the problem.
2. Be flexible on identifying the main categories of causes to the problem. Don't limit categories to the four M's.
3. List all the categories on the main arrow.
4. Brainstorm all possible causes under each category, one at a time.
5. When causes seem to fit in more than one category, place them in all applicable categories, and evaluate which category would make more sense to keep it in based on the impact to solve the problem.
6. Expand each branch for each category and causal factors that may affect the main category as twigs on each branch of the diagram.

7. Eliminate the ideas that everyone agrees would not cause the problem.

8. Analyze the identified causes to determine the most likely root cause(s).

9. Determine the level of effort to work on the root causes, and plan accordingly.

The advantage of this tool is that you can easily tell when not all the potential causes have been captured; if the completed diagram has only five or six causes, it is incomplete. Too simple a diagram indicates that knowledge of the process or problem is still too shallow, and that further discussion is required. Overall, the cause-and-effect diagram is easy to use and promotes structure while allowing creativity. The disadvantage of the technique is that when individuals don't have enough experience facilitating the conversation around the tool, then only possible causes are found rather than actual root causes.

Developing Corrective Actions

After the problem-solving team has determined and verified the root cause, they need to define a plan of action and determine how to tackle the problem. A corrective action plan is a step-by-step guideline for implementing countermeasures and scheduling corrective processes to achieve targeted outcomes for resolution of identified process errors in the RCA. The plan ensures accountability for the implementation of the corrective actions, which includes follow-up and/or review of the system that evaluates the effectiveness of the corrective actions, and it eliminates repeated deficient practices. Having a corrective action plan in place is necessary to minimize or eliminate undesirable issues detected as root causes. These are a series of initiatives or tests of changes that must be linked to the root cause, working in harmony to keep the issue from recurring. It's always helpful for individuals to keep in mind specific, measurable, attainable, relevant, and timely criteria when setting the corrective actions and measuring progress toward them.

A corrective action must be *specific* and as clear as possible so that the execution owner or team understands the activities necessary to achieve it. The following questions should be addressed to ensure the corrective action is specific: What is the impact and the expectation you want to achieve by implementing the action? Where? When? How? What resources are needed? Is there any limitation?

Measurable is the next criteria. How does the problem-solving team measure success? Each corrective action must be tracked and measured to monitor progress and determine if the problem recurrence stops. Similarly, the action must be *attainable* so that the problem-solving team stays motivated and focused, knowing that the desired outcome is possible.

Relevant and timely are the last two criteria. The problem-solving team should be aware of the impact and the possible implication that a corrective action could have on the problem it is intended to solve. Also, setting an expectation of a completion date is important; the execution team must determine a reasonable period in which they can complete the action.

Considering these criteria while defining corrective actions strengthens the plan and gives the problem-solving team direction to refer to when it is time to assess whether or not the test of changes was successful.

The plan should be used as a guide to ensure compliance with quality requirements. This is possible when each corrective action includes an owner, status, estimated completion date, and desired outcome, among others. Each corrective action must be identified by assigning an Action ID—a succinct description of the action required to mitigate the deficiency, found by referring to the policy, manual, guidance, work instruction, standard work, or any other existing documentation (if applicable) in which the process is deficient. The owner is the individual accountable for the execution of the test of change and a status that identifies the current state of the implementation. Each action should have a start date, expected completion date, and a percentage indicating the extent to which each step is complete (i.e., 25%, 50%, 75%, and 100%).

The action plan should consider the people elements, which includes emphasizing teamwork, continuous improvement (CI), and celebrating success. The problem-solving team must consider ideas from the individuals who are getting the job done every day in the area proposed for improvement. The frontline staff always come with the best ideas for improving a process. These staff members should be suggesting and implementing corrective actions not only for the work they do, but also from the perspective that only they possess.

The following questions may help the problem-solving team generate a corrective action plan:

1. Did you involve the team in developing the corrective actions?
2. Do corrective actions address the root cause? How do you know?

3. How will you communicate your plan to encourage trust and engagement?
4. What is the impact of each corrective action?
5. Has there been discussion with the implementation team about what was learned and what is next?
6. How will the team adjust if the process and/or outcome does not meet expected results?

The corrective action plan serves the purpose of a record of a small test of changes to close or at least reduce the gap defined in the problem statement. It is important not to implement more than two corrective actions at the same time. Executing multiple corrective actions simultaneously may impede the team in identifying which action was effective in terms of addressing the issue and reaching the goal. Nonetheless, the team may face some challenges when prioritizing which corrective action should be implemented first. Determining the corrective action to implement first benefits the team's engagement, communication, and the success of the problem-solving initiative. There are two consensus development techniques that I recommend to problem-solving teams prioritizing corrective actions: (1) the Nominal Group Technique, and (2) the Delphi Technique.

The Nominal Group Technique

The nominal group technique is an evaluative methodology for group decision-making processes. It was developed by Andrew H. Van de Ven and Andre L. Delbecq. This technique is well-known due to its effectiveness in ensuring the equitable involvement of every participant, and it results in a set of prioritized recommendations.

The technique includes four stages: (1) silent brainstorming, (2) round-robin, (3) clarification, and (4) voting. Once the corrective actions are identified and defined, the problem-solving facilitator needs to make sure all team members understand each of the actions. Then, the nominal group technique exercise can begin by having each team member generate and write down on a sticky note the attributes for each action. The facilitator proceeds to collect all sticky notes and sort them for each action. The round-robin stage starts with each team member discussing each attribute for clarification, discarding or eliminating those attributes that are similar or serve the same purpose. This elimination process must happen via consensus. Then, each member selects five attributes, evaluates them, and anonymously ranks them to gain a hierarchy according to importance. Individuals should assign a number value to the ranking from five for the most important to one for the least important attribute. Finally, the facilitator collects the rankings from everyone to determine which action received the highest-ranking score, indicating the team's consensus as to the priority of executing each action in the plan.

The Delphi Technique

I always emphasize that the problem-solving team should include the subject matter expert in the area under assessment. These are individuals who are directly related to the system, process, or tasks that support the area affected by the problem. Having experts postulating their own ideas or theories about a course of action to eliminate a problem's root cause makes the decision-making process a difficult hurdle to overcome in coming to a consensus. Oftentimes, I find experts showing resistance to adapting other people's ideas because they tend to be focused on their own reasons, opinions, and points of view. Therefore, by using the Delphi technique, one can overcome this situation due to its reliable group communication structure; it allows a group to reach a consensus in any decision-making venture.

The Delphi technique consists of interactive rounds, as many as necessary, where participants anonymously fill in a primary questionnaire containing questions on the examined issue to yield a consensus. The first step is to develop a questioner. A questioner should be prepared by either the facilitator or by both facilitator and subject matter experts to present the issues marked by a divergence of opinions. In this case, where actions in the corrective action plan are defined and prioritization is the issue, the questioner should present arguments to support those actions that should be implemented first. Once the questioner is established, then the first round begins by having each participant anonymously reviewing, addressing, and responding or commenting. These responses are collected by the facilitator to summarize the top answers, between three and five in number, to send back to all responders before the second round. At this point, participants would be able to review and discuss their comments. This exercise gives participants the opportunity to reflect on their answers versus other people's points of view. The key here is to have everybody replying anonymously to avoid the influence of the other individuals' opinions. Then, participants are asked to rank the top answers, and a second round of questions is developed based on the ranking selection and the additional information learned from the first-round discussion. Another iteration is ready to begin, and participants may continue to do even more until a pattern of consensus emerges or they obtain views on possible strategies to execute the corrective action plan.

The problem-solving team must ensure corrective actions are linked to a root cause and monitor if a systematic implementation has a satisfactory impact in stopping cause recurrence.

Monitoring Results

Monitoring corrective action via visual management is a continuing function that provides process stakeholders with an ongoing intervention that includes early indications of progress, and improves the effectiveness of communication and reaction. The purpose is to detect changes as they occur in the process and ensure that improvements continue to meet targets and goals over a specific period.

A monitoring plan is critical to the success of the problem-solving initiative. Corrective actions performance must be measured to understand and ascertain whether expectations and targets have been met. If expectations and targets are not met, then the problem-solving team should make the decision to either adjust or desist and move on to the next corrective action. Once the corrective action plan is agreed upon, the problem-solving team must figure out and understand the control system to be used to ensure that the action plan is carried out. A monitoring plan specifies key performance indicators (KPIs) and how often they will be tracked; the method of quality control and data gathering, recording, and reporting; and who will be accountable to adjust and/or adapt process changes. This not only gives the problem-solving team actionable data, but it will also provide actionable information through focused reporting that is available anytime. The metrics are KPIs that translate the action plan into performance standards and must be measurable, achievable, and clear. A properly identified and executed metric along with the right communication feedback loop can yield immeasurable benefits to the problem-solving initiative.

A well-known monitoring tool that employs statistical methods to control a process is the statistical process control (SPC) chart. SPC is a visual tool displaying data information over time. Its purpose is to use statistical methods to depict variation in a process. When executing corrective actions, SPC charts will help the team to monitor and identify variations or anomalies throughout the implementation process. Variation can come from differences in sources such as supplies, equipment functionality, people skills, and the way a process is performed. The key here is the ability of the problem-solving team to distinguish between measurement variation and process variation. Measurement variation relates to accuracy, consistency, and stability, while process variation is due to standardization. The goal is to evaluate to what extent variation exists in the process when a corrective action has been executed to eliminate the root cause.

The main tool in SPC is the control chart. Control charts depict process performance by plotting data points with predetermined control limits (see Figure 19 and Figure 20). Process owners can benefit from this tool by monitoring how the

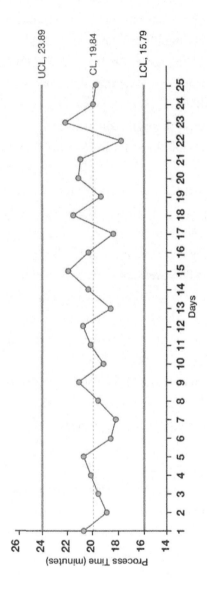

Figure 19: Control chart showing how a random process cycle time in minutes changes over time Sample of a control chart where the arithmetic mean cycle time is 19.840 minutes as the centerline (CL), the upper control limit (UCL) is 23.890 minutes, and the lower control limit (LCL) is 15.790 minutes. It can be determined that the random process is stable since all cycle times observed for 25 days are between the tolerable boundaries (UCL and LCL) established.

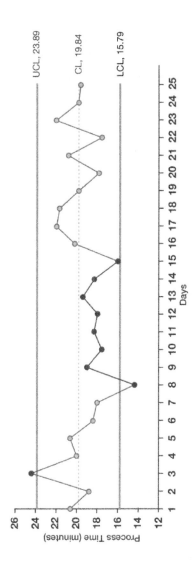

Figure 20: Control chart showing an unstable random process cycle time in minutes

Control chart example showing data points (red dots) outside of the control limits and/or three or more successive data points on the same side of the centerline

data behaves within the control limits and if there is any shift in the process. Finally, a process is in statistical control when the statistical properties do not vary over time. A control chart includes a scatter plot presenting a view of how the process changes over time with upper and lower control limits.

Creating a control chart consists of the ability to determine the arithmetic mean and the standard deviation. The arithmetic mean represents the center or middle of the data, and the standard deviation is the spread, or the data variation, in a sample or a population. These two statistics measure whether the problem-solving team can create a control chart after examining if the data is normally distributed. Assuming that the data is distributed normally, then the team calculates one standard deviation above and below the arithmetic mean. One standard deviation means that 68.3% of all data is considered. Similarly, two and three standard deviations above and below the arithmetic means include 95.4% and 99.7%, respectively, of all the data in the data set as illustrated in Figure 21. Finally, after calculating the arithmetic mean and all three plus and minus standard deviations, the problem-solving team can construct the control chart. The third plus and minus standard deviations represent the upper and lower control limits, respectively. The control limits in the control chart represent the boundaries of a process variation, and any value outside of the plus or minus boundaries helps to identify when the process is out of control.

Monitoring the performance of the corrective actions includes adding data to the control chart to ensure enough information is available to identify any variations and shifts within the process. A huge challenge for the problem-solving team is the team's tendency to interpret results as confirmation

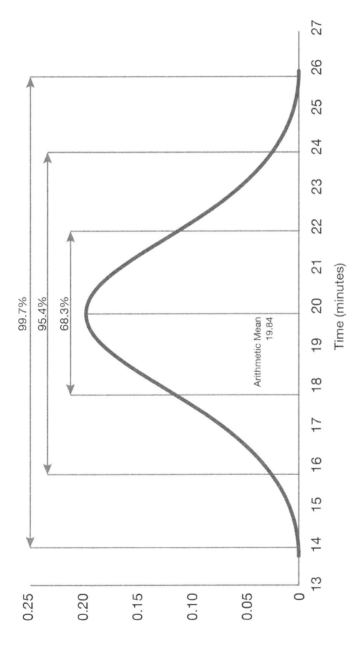

Figure 21: Normal distribution of the random process time in minutes from Figure 19

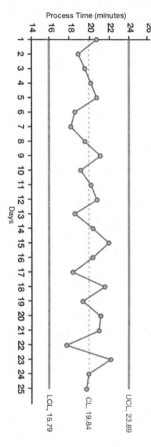

Figure 22: Control chart and normal distribution relationship
The control limits of the control chart are at +1 and -1 standard deviation and the centerline reflects the center of the distribution of the time in minutes for the random processes. The data set behaves in normality patterns since all data points lie within ±1 standard deviation.

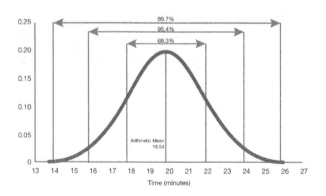

of their root cause hypotheses or beliefs. In other words, the team should not analyze the results with a desired outcome in mind. Oftentimes, a team can be so immersed in the problem-solving process that it is difficult to shift their mindset toward acceptance when the data is telling them something new. The control chart cannot provide enough information to conclude why the process has variation; it can only display the presence of the variation.

Annotating, commenting, and visualizing the presence of the variation is a good practice while monitoring outcomes in order to explain the steps taken throughout implementing corrective actions. This information is important to demonstrate performance of corrective actions and to ensure processes are consistent. Moreover, this information can provide insight to make adjustments before they become a problem. If the corrective action has not addressed the root cause, then adjust as necessary, review lessons learned with all individuals responsible for implementing the action plan, and provide feedback.

Once the problem-solving team is ready to review what has worked well and what has not, then the team should be able to identify what is unique and different about the impact the corrective action had on the root cause. The team should consider what has changed, if anything, to give rise to the improvement and record when changes occurred.

IMPROVEMENT

The goal here is to determine how to implement optimization as a particularly appropriate application for the problem-solving process. There are numerous improvement approaches to standardize activities and business processes. However, to be a practical tool, improvement must be integrated into the problem-solving process. The process improvement community has emphasized some approaches, such as 5S, Waste Elimination, Continuous Improvement, RACI, Mistake-Proofing, and Cost-Benefit Analysis. Implementing and adapting any of these approaches requires knowledge, commitment, discipline, and great communication to avoid indecision, misdirection, or weak interpretation. The success of optimizing your business process relies on consistently using any of the approaches selected for your initiative, measuring the improvements, refining, and making sure that the approach becomes part of the organization's culture.

Waste Elimination

The concept of waste elimination was first introduced by Taiichi Ohno, an industrial engineer and manager at Toyota Motor

Corporation. He is also known for his work and the development of the Toyota Production System. The Toyota Production System is based on the philosophy of elimination of all nonvalue-added activities, also known as waste, to make the vehicle assembly operation more efficient.

After many years of improvement attempts and CI implementations, Ohno identified the seven most frequent types of waste: defects, waiting, inventory, transportation, motion, overproduction, and overprocessing. Later, these business process activities became popular and noticeable in other organizations besides the auto industry. Some organizations even added an eighth waste: talent. Organizations began adopting initiatives to eliminate these wastes within their operations and adapting the "lean" methodology with the objective of reducing operational costs and optimizing resources.

Waste identification could be a part of the result of a RCA. Think about it: almost any inefficiency or challenge you face in your work environment could be categorized as any of the eight wastes. Keep in mind that the inefficiencies in your organization are counted as part of overhead, increasing the operational costs. These are costs that none of the potential customers will be willing to pay extra for because of the inability to control and streamline the processes. However, optimization is included as part of the toolbox. The problem-solving team can implement a mechanism during the corrective action to proactively identify whether any of the inefficiencies are associated with these nonvalue-added activities. Also, the problem-solving team should be aware that most of the time, these wastes are directly related to miscommunication or something not properly handed off throughout the business process.

For example, how would each of these wastes apply to supply change and administrative processes? The team should be able to understand how these wastes are expressed as symptoms of a potential problem that results in an additional cost to business operations.

1. <u>Defects/Errors</u>: Any activity that results in unsatisfied customers or causes delays, quantity errors, billing errors, inventory discrepancies and adjustments, damage of goods, or rework.

2. <u>Waiting/Delay</u>: Any idle time within a process. This could be any person waiting to receive a service or any item, information, or material waiting to be processed. Waiting for a meeting to start, and information systems downtime are common examples.

3. <u>Inventory</u>: Storing excess items not planned. Any raw materials stored, excessive work in process, unsold finished goods, and unread emails are some examples of the waste of inventory. Unnecessary inventory can be built up by procuring or acquiring more items than needed, receiving raw materials in advance, and shipping final goods late.

4. <u>Transportation</u>: Unnecessary transport and handling of goods or materials from point A to point B that results in added cost.

5. <u>Motion</u>: Unnecessary movement of people, usually more than three feet, including walking, reaching, and stretching. A symptom of this waste can be identified by detecting poor layout in the workstation. Example: walking to a printer, or from office to office.

6. Overproduction: Generating information or making products before needed; producing more than what the next step/process or workstation can handle. This waste unbalances your operation, resulting in unreliable process building up inventory.

7. Overprocessing: Unnecessary steps that are not required and do not compromise the work quality, adding cost to your operation, i.e., inspection processes when not needed, or approval requests that provide no real value. Tracking unnecessary information, generating unnecessary reports and copies, or calling for meetings in which the information could be put in an email are other examples. Avoiding combining steps when doing so makes more sense.

8. Talent: Underutilizing staff capabilities, or delegating tasks without adequate training.

Continuous Improvement

The concepts of CI have been around for a long time. This is a progressive improvement sometimes focused on either working conditions or performance metrics related to processes to eliminate waste and increase customer satisfaction and financial benefits. CI is also known as *Kaizen*, which is the Japanese word for "improvement." There are some improvement approaches that can be related to improvements, such as Lean Methodology, Six Sigma, the blend of Lean and Six Sigma (Lean Six Sigma), Total Quality Management, and Process Re-Engineering, among others. Even though all of these have their own systematic applications and techniques, they are improvement approaches adapted by organizations to support events with the goal of analyzing how the current work is done in order to make it better.

The CI events usually take between one and two weeks. Individuals in CI events can obtain quick results related to waste elimination, better customer service, process through-put improvement, lower cost, improved safety, cost avoidance, and better product and service quality. Notice that CI is often applied as part of a corrective action through a consistent and sustained plan. The implementation of a consistent action plan can result in a truly effective CI.

Typically, a CI event begins with visiting the area desired for improvement to make direct observations and to interview those individuals directly related to the process. Witnessing how the work is done and understanding the actual challenges people are facing will provide the necessary background to set the goal for the CI event. Once all observations are completed, a process map can be developed to capture the current process. Similar steps from the section entitled UNDERSTAND-ING are useful for mapping the process. The map will provide enough information to develop the CI plan and to prioritize corrective actions or tests of change. Then, the team should proceed to implement the action plan and report on the results. Finally, the team loops back to the defined goal to validate if the improvements closed the gap to meet the established goal.

Once the improvement event is concluded, make sure that the changes made do not affect customer requirements or any team, department, or unit within the organization. Also, ensure that the changes made have the structure and support from the leadership to be sustained. A failure mode of CI events occurs when people or the leadership go back to operating the way things were in the past, due to change considerations (resistance), lack of communication, or misunderstanding.

The CI approach is as good as the people and the leadership involved want it to be. It must be clear that these CI events aim to reduce process variation by creating standardized processes. Also, a change management framework must be integrated as the complement of any CI event supporting leadership and people involved in the process.

5S

The 5S methodology is a standardized process to reduce waste and optimize productivity that creates and maintains an organized, safe, and efficient workplace. It was first originated and implemented by Toyota Motors Corporation in postwar Japan (1945). This methodology is considered part of the Lean philosophy to support CI and waste elimination initiatives that consist of five steps, whereby each step starts with the letter S in Japanese: *seiri, seiton, seiso, seiketsu,* and *shitsuke.* These are: sort, set in order, shine, standardize, and sustain, respectively.

Let's assume that you need to organize your closet at home. You want to be able to find your garments quickly without wasting time searching for them. The end goal requires identifying what's necessary and what isn't by eliminating those outfits that you don't wear anymore, cleaning the shelving, sorting the hanging space, putting things in order, and figuring out a routine for keeping the closet organized on a regular basis.

A similar activity applies to the workspace. Everything in the work area should have a designated place. When the work area is well organized, it is easier to identify when essential work items and tools are missing or misplaced. This is the crucial advantage of visual management as part of the 5S methodology, which aims to minimize time spent looking for tools and items to perform the work, as well as to reduce excessive motion.

A 5S implementation would result in the following:

Sort. Eliminate unnecessary items from the workplace. The sorting exercise gives visibility to space availability and enables one to eliminate or put away unwanted things. Back to the closet example: select those unused outfits that are old or you dislike wearing. These items are moved away from the closet so that you can assess each clothing piece and each accessory and then deal with them appropriately.

Set in Order. Arrange items so that they are easy to find and use. Straightening all necessary items in the workspace is critical to creating an efficient and effective storage method. For instance, in the closet example, a strategy to *set in order* includes: repainting, selecting hanger types, customizing the storage concept, building shoe holders, outlining locations, and arranging clothing items by color or, the way I prefer to do, by type (such as short and long sleeves, button-down shirts, knit shirts, etc.).

Shine. Determine the routine to keep workplace areas clean and orderly. Maintaining a clean environment and keeping a work area organized give workers the opportunity to notice equipment malfunction or failures and react more quickly. For example, consider having your closet constantly looking sharp to minimize the time you have to spend cleaning the area and searching for outfits to wear.

Standardize. Establish and follow a standard way for organization and processes. These include: documenting, standard operating procedures, standard work, work instruction, job aids, checklists, or roles and responsibilities. In this fourth step, you should also come up with a standard process to avoid accumulation of unneeded items. In other words, know how to prevent the reformed work area from going back to the way it was at step 1. For your reorganized closet, create a standard that encompasses designated places for clothes, shoes, and accessories.

Sustain. Make steps 3 and 4 (shine and standardize) a daily routine. Having the discipline to walk the talk, to follow the standard and turn this new practice into habit will help to avoid a return to the original way of doing things. The purpose of this step is to ingrain the 5S methodology into the culture of the organization. This is the most difficult part because it requires a change in management and training, as well as support from upper management. For your closet: make sure to periodically update it by identifying and discarding unused outfits and accessories in a bid to keep the area clean, fun, and easy to navigate.

There are some organizations that have adapted a sixth S for safety, also known as 5S + 1. Safety is critical in any work environment. This means making sure that every individual has the right training, resources, and information available to perform tasks as expected. The objective is to foster a work environment that enhances safety by having clutter-free working spaces and identifying hazards in order to reduce the risk of accidents.

Responsibility Charting

Cross-functional dynamics is very common in the modern business environment where teams have to conduct and collaborate in different tasks. Even if the leadership in the organization hasn't acknowledged it, the cross-functional environment exists. Cross-functional teams working toward the same goal, where members have different skill sets, will eventually collide if their roles and responsibilities are not well defined. Most likely, team members will begin to step on each other's toes, not understanding their responsibilities, work boundaries, and accountabilities. Oftentimes, these issues create situations where there is lack of trust, blame when targets are not met, wasted time, inaction on decisions, and a team that is overwhelmed. These are symptoms of a lack of communication and understanding about which roles and responsibilities each team member will take on in a problem-solving initiative.

Adopting a responsibility charting tool will help teams to document and understand their roles and responsibilities by keeping team members on the same page. This tool creates a simple table illustrating essential information to keep your team focused and on track. This means that the team will be able to make decisions faster, have knowledge of where to get input and feedback, and obtain a good understanding of accountability.

There are many versions of responsibility charting; however, the responsible, accountable, consult, and inform (RACI) matrix is the simplest and most common.

- Responsible: Are team members responsible for completing tasks and making decisions related to an activity?
- Accountable: The individual who must approve when an activity or a task is completed or a decision has been made.
- Consult: Any individual or team that needs to provide input or feedback before a task or activity is completed or a decision is made. Most likely, the consulted figure is a subject matter expert.
- Inform: Any individual or team that needs to receive a progress status report.

How to develop a RACI chart:

1. Identify all the steps or activities required to be met in a defined goal or objective. These are the must-do, can't-fail activities in the order they need to be accomplished.
2. Identify all stakeholders required and involved in making these activities successful.
3. Create a chart, placing all activities (from step 1) in rows on the left side and the stakeholders as headings in columns.
4. Fill in the RACI chart, identifying who is responsible and accountable for each activity. The chart must include one accountable stakeholder for each activity and one or more people responsible.

5. Complete the chart by identifying stakeholders to be consulted and informed.
6. Review each activity and resolve overlaps, if applicable.
7. Share the RACI chart with all stakeholders and obtain their agreement and approval. If necessary, resolve any discrepancies.

It is important to thoroughly analyze the RACI chart with all stakeholders to make sure everybody understands their roles and responsibilities. Having everybody on the same page ensures that communication is effective. While sharing the RACI chart, make sure that no stakeholder is missing. Agree that at least one person is responsible for getting the activity done or for making a decision. Watch out for the consulted segment; too many consulted stakeholders might slow down the process, creating waste. Confirm that the work is balanced among those stakeholders assigned as being responsible. Can any responsible stakeholder be changed to a consult or vice versa? Can any who consult be changed to informed status or vice versa?

Responsibility charting is a powerful tool to assign accountability, set expectations, and manage communication in any project initiative.

A simple example of responsibility charting would be for a rock band playing at a music venue (see Table 9).

Mistake-Proofing

We all make mistakes, and business processes are not exempt from any kind of failure mode. Accidents are the most common events caused by failure mode contributing factors. For

Table 9: RACI Matrix

ID	Activities/ Tasks	Rock Band	Band Manager	Venue Manager	Lights Technician	Sound Technician
1	Contract agreement	A	R	R	-	-
2	Ticket sales	I	A	R	-	-
3	Playlist selection	R	A	-	C	C
4	Venue readiness	C	I	A	R	R
5	Band practice playlist	R	A	I	C	C
6	Showtime	R	A	I	R	R

instance, inadequate training, poor decisions, or inattention are some factors that lead to disasters. The mistake-proofing concept prevents individuals from making mistakes throughout any process.

This concept was originated by Shigeo Shingo while he established quality standards as an integral part of the Toyota Production System implemented at Toyota Motor Corporation. The Japanese term for mistake-proofing is *Poka Yoke*, a well-known term within the manufacturing industry. Over time, this concept has evolved and adapted in many other ways; we now use it not only to prevent a mistake before it happens, but also to mitigate, detect, facilitate, replace, and eliminate. Mistake-proofing can support any business process in different ways. For instance, it helps with detection and prevention of business process errors, resulting in avoiding costs and increasing quality standards, thereby making the business process more reliable. It contributes to creating a safer work environment for all employees.

How to implement a mistake-proofing mechanism

Identify the activities or places that are more vulnerable to creating any kind of mistake within the work area or the business process. Any activity should have a mechanism to either prevent an error from happening or detect when an error occurs. These mechanisms can serve to control or to warn of mistakes being made.

For instance, a USB cable is designed with a connector that can fit into a slot in a specific orientation and position with precision and accuracy to prevent someone from putting it in the wrong slot. Another example includes the oxygen line in an inpatient room having a valve designed with a specified pin index safety system. This mistake-proofing system prevents the health-care provider from connecting the oxygen line onto another medical gas outlet, such as medical air, nitrous oxide, or the vacuum line.

Similarly, mistake-proofing applies visual management, alerts, and sound systems to avoid inadvertent actions from individuals that could lead to an accident or defect throughout a business process. Think about one of the most common systems you use daily: the road and highway system. A vehicular system applies visual and alert mechanisms to prevent and detect mistakes. For instance, rumble strips on the shoulder of the road cause the vehicle to vibrate roughly, making a loud noise to warn the driver that the vehicle is about to veer off the road. A traffic light is a color-coded visual that alerts drivers as to what action to follow. Pavement markings are also visuals that provide information about road conditions ahead to facilitate the driver's behavior and performance.

Mistake-proofing offers practical applications to improve quality performance and make the business reliable. It helps individuals and business processes get things done right the first time.

Cost-Benefit Analysis

Have you found yourself in the middle of a conversation where people are justifying a course of action based on anecdotes that outweigh its drawbacks? What did you think? Did you go with the flow? After a few hours of discussion, people may start evaluating whether the decision they expect to make is the best decision. What are they doing? Are they considering changing direction or even making a change to the improvement strategy? Do they understand the consequences of making a change? Notice that whenever people discuss pros and cons for a particular situation, they are engaged in a form of cost-benefit analysis.

Cost-benefit analysis is a method that can provide more insight to facilitate your decision-making process. It is a way to evaluate the risk one is willing to take versus the potential benefits that can be gained. For instance, let's consider whether to use a face mask during a viral pandemic. Does the mask only protect the wearer, or does it protect others as well? What are the benefits of wearing the face mask and the risks of not wearing it? The US Center for Disease Control and Prevention advised that since the mask is meant to contain people's germs, preventing them from reaching others, wearing a mask protects both the wearer and others around them. On the other hand, breathing dampens the mask when wearing it for a long time, causing it to lose the protective effect for both the wearer and the environment. This is an example of cost-benefit analysis that is not necessarily a monetary decision.

Monetary or financial decisions can also be analyzed with the cost-benefit methodology and should not be confused with a return of investment analysis. A return of investment analysis helps to determine if an investment is good over time. The cost-benefit analysis assesses the need and opportunity carried out by an initiative. It is a highly efficient methodology in decision-making because it allows for the evaluation of alternatives at the lowest cost or risk.

There are a variety of cost-benefit analysis methods designed to compare the benefits and cost in order to determine and foresee a course of action. The benefit-cost ratio is the methodology covered here where a present value expected from the benefits of an initiative is divided by a present value from the costs of the same initiative. This simple math concept helps to determine the viability from implementing or executing an initiative. Of course, there is heavier math analysis involved; however, the purpose here is to provide a quick glance and a high-level understanding of the rationale behind the methodology and tools available.

Let's assume that the problem-solving team has executed a corrective action that is getting great results on closing the gap and identifying the problem statement. However, the problem-solving team has considered various alternatives to hardwire the corrective action taken to optimize the process, thus requiring some investment and a process redesign.

The problem-solving team identified an extension of the information technology infrastructure that would allow greater network capacity. IT4U, Inc. is a company capable of performing the work required and the only one to provide a quote for the work. IT4U offered bandwidth hardware and software, applications connectivity, maintenance package, and resources, whether on-premises or in the cloud. This solution would require a contract with IT4U of an initial investment of $498,000; then, $17,000 in the first year, $23,000 in the second year, and $175,000 in the third year. The problem-solving team has been informed by the new business and finance team of a business revenue growth of $388,000, and $675,000 in the second year and third year, respectively. Moreover, they informed the problem-solving team to consider a 7.25% rate to discount future cash flow to the present value. In other words, it is a rate of return that represents the risk the organization will take with relation to the investment. How does the team use this information to determine if the investment as suggested by the corrective actions planned will generate incremental value?

First, the problem-solving team should understand that the benefit-cost ratio is obtained by using the following equation:

$$Benefit - Cost\, Ratio = \frac{B}{C} = \left[\frac{B_o + \frac{B_1}{(1+i)} + \frac{B_2}{(1+i)^2} + ... + \frac{B_t}{(1+i)^t}}{C_o + \frac{C_1}{(1+i)} + \frac{C_2}{(1+i)^2} + ... + \frac{C_t}{(1+i)^t}} \right]$$

Where

B = total benefits; $B_o + \dfrac{B_1}{(1+i)} + \dfrac{B_2}{(1+i)^2} + ... + \dfrac{B_t}{(1+i)^t}$; summation of benefits in each year (t)

t = period of time (i.e., days, weeks, months, quarters, years)

i = discount rate

C = total costs; $C_o + \dfrac{C_1}{(1+i)} + \dfrac{C_2}{(1+i)^2} + ... + \dfrac{C_t}{(1+i)^t}$; summation of costs in each year (t)

Considering the information above, calculate the discounted benefits for each year, and sum the total discounted benefits for the initiative. Similarly, calculate the discounted costs. See Table 10.

Then divide the total discounted benefits over total discounted costs.

$$Benefit - Cost\, Ratio = \frac{B}{C} = ABS\left(\frac{\$884,473}{-\$675,702}\right) = 1.31$$

Table 10: Discounted costs applying 7.25% rate of return

Year	Costs	Cost Actual Value Formula	Discounted Cost
0	-$498,000	-498,000/(1+7.25%)^0	-$498,000
1	-$17,000	-17,000/(1+7.25%)^1	-$15,851
2	-$23,000	-23,000/(1+7.25%)^2	-$19,996
3	-$175,000	-175,000/(1+7.25%)^3	-$141,855
Total			-$675,702

Benefits	Benefit Actual Value Formula	Discounted Benefit
$0	0/(1+7.25%)^0	$0
$0	0/(1+7.25%)^1	$0
$388,000	388,000/(1+7.25%)^2	$337,316
$675,000	675,000/(1+7.25%)^3	$547,157
		$884,473

Notice that the benefit-cost ratio is greater than 1, which means that the benefits exceed the costs. If the benefit-cost ratio results in less than 1, then it is suggested not to move forward with the initiative or project under evaluation.

The benefit-cost ratio of 1:31 suggests an attractive return by investing in information technology infrastructure to expand network capacity. The problem-solving team can make an informed decision to strongly advocate for investing in the suggested initiative, since for every dollar invested, the organization can expect $1.31 in benefits generated.

In summary, a cost-benefit analysis is designed to provide relevant information to facilitate a decision-making process. Remember that the application of this method requires legible, understandable, and sufficiently detailed information.

SUSTAINMENT

Sustainment is the last phase in the road map to problem-solving. During this phase, leaders must have an active role because they are routinely expected to support staff's problem-solving. This effort offers the potential to exercise proper oversight; therefore, a sustainment governance model may contribute to managing changes and ensuring that staff has the understanding, motivation, and means to maintain improvements.

Sustainment is poorly understood. It is not a surprise that after a few months working on corrective actions and improvements, we start noticing fatigue from leadership, the problem-solving team, and staff. They might experience or demonstrate quick wins at first, but eventually, they divert their attention to whatever is next on their to-do list. You must prevent everyone from returning to the old ways; doing so might result in staff resistance toward later improvement initiatives.

The objective is to coach the staff and the organization into the habit of problem-solving thinking that influences changes by creating patterns for daily improvement and impacting the organization's performance. I suggest you engage leadership to take an active role in this phase by holding people accountable and developing a model that includes standardization, performance metrics, and routine check-in meetings.

Standardization

Any business today is under pressure to deliver products or services more efficiently while responding to a customer's demands. The key to overcome this constant challenge or complex problem is to find a better way to manage businesses with the least possible variations. That is correct! We must aim to have no variation while running the business. Standard guidance must be defined for every critical business process.

Imagine a principal road in your neighborhood without signalization and traffic laws to follow. How would you safely drive? Not having the ability to maintain a certain level of traffic discipline results in variability in driver behavior, such as speeding, adequate sharing of space, and traffic flow, causing the road to quickly fill with collisions. It would be total chaos. Transportation laws, regulations, and uniform signage provide safety and security, order, and guidance to drivers, cyclists, and pedestrians. Similarly, standardization ensures uniformity to certain practices once changes occur in the business process. Having standard processes helps the staff to set expectations and to define activities in order to consistently achieve the desired results. Also, standardized processes smooth the learning process for new staff, make possible comparative measures of performance for future changes, and facilitate regulatory audits.

Once the problem-solving team has cracked the code and identified which corrective actions are sustainable, then the organization needs a set of standards to sustain such improvements. Documenting all standards promotes consistency in the business process of accomplishing a particular objective for a particular customer, either internal or external, indicating best practices to conduct processes and the metrics to measure performance. The staff must be aware of the existence of a standard work document and have access to the document that they are expected to follow. Leaders must ensure that every business process stakeholder understands and follows the document by facilitating periodic reviews and allowing the staff to identify opportunities to improve the procedure. If leaders or the problem-solving team observe staff who are not following the standard work documentation, then they should understand the challenges and difficulties the staff is experiencing; they should provide more training and reinforce the importance of maintaining consistency in the business process.

It is important to avoid adding a layer to the organization's bureaucracy by loading in a bunch of unnecessary procedure documentations. Focus your effort on documenting exactly what the staff needs to successfully complete the work. More importantly, the standard documentation must be developed by the staff who do the work with the guidance from the problem-solving team and subject-matter experts. The staff doing the work have the best knowledge and insight. Avoid ignoring frontline staff's feedback and input by having a group of outsiders develop the standard work document.

What type of documentation works best to record a standard process, increasing efficiency while avoiding variability? Before determining what type of documentation works best, be aware of any laws, regulations, or policies that rule your business. It is very important that you consult someone in the organization who knows well what regulates your business; whatever documentation you develop should not go against any regulation. For instance, patient care is constantly improving and evolving, even though the health-care industry is highly regulated. However, patient care improvement cannot bypass or supersede any health and safety policies.

Different types of documentation or a documentation hierarchy usually exist within any organization, such as policies, manuals, standard operating procedures, work instructions, job aids, records, and forms. However, here I will cover standard operating procedures, work instructions, or job aids to document your standardized process that must be accessible all the time to the staff conducting the jobs. Procedures include the purpose, scope, and responsibilities of all process stakeholders. A procedure describes the best practice of completing a process in either a narrative form or through diagrams and flowcharts. It also can refer to any relevant tool, work instruction, job aid, or checklist to help achieve the desired outcome. Work instructions involve more detailed documentation than procedures. Instructions must include the content of activities in a sequenced order from beginning to end, estimated time to perform each activity, and who is assigned to complete each activity. Similarly, work instructions can be documented in either a narrative form or through diagrams and flowcharts. Job aids aim to provide supplemental information and clear details of how to execute an activity to reduce avoidable mistakes. They usually include graphic information or pictures printed as a one-pager or cheat sheet posted right where the job is being done. Job aids are especially beneficial as a memory jogger for those activities or tasks that change frequently, and to help staff remember what they learned from training.

In summary, documenting all standards implies that the staff involved in a process needs to change its behavior to sustain improvements while ensuring that the quality of products or services is always the same. The staff doing the work and the organization will experience less variation on process tasks and activities that lead to poorer outcomes, driving up costs and frustrating staff. This offers the opportunity to maintain better communications about how the business process operates, enable smooth handoffs across process boundaries, and improve performance.

Key Performance Indicators (KPIs)

Organizations use KPIs to manage and communicate results. These KPIs allow leaders and staff to determine to what extent their strategic plans are being implemented. However, over the years, databases and information repositories have increased massively, resulting in better access to information and data overload. In a fast-paced business environment where an informed decision is made based on data analytics, leaders and staff can be overloaded with information. People may search for key data or decide to start collecting new information to measure performance. The question I must ask is, are leaders and problem-solving teams identifying and defining the right KPIs? By identifying and defining KPIs, I mean indicators that can accurately pinpoint whether activities or business processes are having a direct impact on the organization's target and goal. What is the indicator to inform performance? What type of data is needed to measure performance? Is the indicator aligned to the business objective? How are the activities or processes observed to inform data? Can these activities or processes be measured accurately? When and how often is the data collected? What is the source of the data? Is it by direct observation or technology systems? Who is accountable for collecting the data? Who is accountable for analyzing and interpreting the data? Are staff comfortable collecting or gathering the data? Finally, is it a lagging or leading indicator? All these questions must be addressed to ensure we have the right information directed toward an intended result.

For instance, let us assume that you want to lose twenty pounds in the next six months. The metric is straightforward: body weight in pounds. Now, do you consider body weight in pounds a lagging or leading indicator? How often do you plan to measure it? How would you measure it? What does the weight in pounds inform? Is just measuring body weight enough to inform how we are achieving the goal? Is this metric enough to inform what course of action is needed when the metric is trending in the wrong direction? These are some of the questions that you need to address when identifying what kind of metrics you will use to measure your performance toward achieving the goal of losing twenty pounds in six months.

In this example, I consider the body weight in pounds as a lagging indicator because it tends to have a delayed reaction. It would inform the result of other activities that must be executed other than just hopping on the scale every morning to monitor how many pounds you have lost from the previous day. To lose weight, you may have visited your primary care physician for guidance and advice on a weight-loss plan. Let's assume that the plan includes a gym exercise routine and a dietary plan for weight loss. Identifying metrics to measure the success following this plan are the leading indicators. Consider leading indicators as measurable factors that change the old habit of doing things to follow a desired trend. In other words, these are the metrics that drive the body weight in the pounds indicator. The number of calories per day in our diets, along with other factors, can be used to predict the changes in body weight. For instance, by measuring calories consumed, calories burned, and gym routine, daily information will be provided about body weight tendency. Do not expect to see significant weight loss if you do not stick with the dietary plan or show up at the gym. Therefore, lagging and leading indicators are a set of performance measures that detect when metrics are not trending in the right direction at an early stage of their occurrence, allowing teams to respond immediately to those issues that impede reaching a desired goal. In other words, make sure that indicators address the gap that is intended to be closed between the current situation and the desired target performance.

I have met many teams that struggle to identify the right KPI. Some of them struggle because the culture of measuring performance constantly is inexistent. There are teams that simply do not understand the need to measure performance. Other teams struggle because they experience fear of judgment, or they believe that they would be punished by reporting current performances. Also, I have witnessed teams taking shortcuts on identifying measurements that constantly fall into the green zone and are not necessarily aligned with a strategy. These teams intend to show how well they are doing and want to demonstrate that their business processes are under control. However, when rigorously evaluating the indicators, we find that they are not even aligned with the business objective, impeding the team and leadership from identifying what critical adjustments are required to meet the business goals. It is highly desirable that you advise teams and leadership about how to identify indicators that are relevant and able to demonstrate progress toward the business goal.

Well-defined KPIs inform the sorts of challenges teams are facing and what hurdles they need to overcome to achieve their goal. They are a communication tool to inform leadership when things need to be escalated and to identify the support the team needs from the organization. By no means should KPIs be punitive toward staff, negatively impacting their morale. I always advise leaders to create a stress-free and pressure-free work environment in which the staff feels safe to show process defects and mistakes while getting support to learn from them. I encourage teams to display metrics showing current situations and to be comfortable when metrics are in red (indicators trending in the opposite direction). This helps with accountability and promotes an honest conversation among staff about things that are working well and not so well. In addition, this helps to facilitate the process of identifying support from the organization and opportunities for improvement.

How to determine what to measure:

1. Ensure your team fully understands what the business objective is.
2. Discuss with the team and leadership how your division, unit, or team contributes to achieve the goals that drive the business objective.

3. Identify the activities or processes that have a direct impact on achieving those goals.

4. Brainstorm with the team, including leadership, on how to measure the success for the activities or processes in Step 3. Make sure the team does not come up with measures or prescriptive metrics that other teams are currently implementing. Each process, activity, and task is unique.

5. Define the indicator to measure success from Step 4. This would be the lagging metric.

6. Identify the critical tasks required for the processes to be successful.

7. Define the indicator to measure success from Step 6. This would be the leading metric.

8. Determine what type of information or data is required to measure the leading metric.

9. Ensure that the number of metrics is not too large and overwhelming for the team to maintain. Focus only on critical tasks.

10. Determine how often the information or data will be gathered.

11. Assign roles and responsibilities within the team to collect, record, and maintain data.

12. Decide on the requirements for documenting and reporting each measure.

13. Establish targets and thresholds describing the desired performance level. Consider this step as the reference point to measure success.

14. Ensure the team understands and feels comfortable with the indicators, and determine how data is interpreted.

15. Describing desired performance levels is as important as selecting the measure.

Accountability

Leaders who comprehend the technical skills involved in solving problems are better suited to support the workforce in any given improvement initiative. Having regular check-ins with staff is an effective practice to understand firsthand what is going well and the kinds of challenges they are facing that impede them from being successful. This practice, properly executed, clearly demonstrates the leadership's commitment to support problem-solving teams during improvement initiatives while promoting a culture of problem-solving in the organization. This routine is a way for leaders to walk the talk. It is a golden opportunity to encourage the contributions of those they lead in order to strengthen improvements.

The purpose of meaningful check-ins is to obtain actionable information and to reinforce accountability. Accountability is a critical two-way street to justify any action. The staff assumes the responsibility of doing their best to accomplish their goals, and leaders suit up staff with the necessary tools and continuous support to help them to be successful. When having meaningful check-ins with staff, the goal is to build a foundation of trust with the staff, increase feedback, and to learn about their thought processes toward improvements.

Leaders who wish to have their problem-solving team be successful at implementing improvement must have an active participation themselves supporting the team. They must embrace their approach, enabling frontline staff to lead the improvements. However, they might experience the staff pointing fingers elsewhere or even hiding results when the desired outcome is not reached. Most likely, this behavior is noticeable in an environment that lacks trust and where consequences are levied. Nevertheless, if leaders are humble and fair, and they acknowledge their contribution to the staff's failure, the staff are more likely to be honest. When the staff believe that leaders are consistent at the check-in meeting, interested in their learning experience, and less focused on punitive actions, they tend to feel less inclined to hide their underperformance and are eager to tell their stories of achievement and struggles. As staff tell their stories, leaders will begin feeling more comfortable offering feedback and coaching. Leadership must be sure to cover the following:

1. What are we trying to achieve?
2. How are we doing today? (Review latest KPIs and data.)
3. What course of action was taken since the last check-in?
4. What is working well?
5. Who has been helpful?
6. What have staff learned from the process since the last check-in?
7. Does the staff have the tools and equipment to do their jobs?
8. What team, action, or system can be working better?
9. What are the challenges that the staff are facing?
10. Are the staff using appropriate decision-making methods/ tools?
11. Discuss what, if anything, can be done differently.
12. Discuss the next steps and the expected outcome.

13. What does the staff need from leadership?
14. Are timelines realistic?
15. When was the last time success was celebrated?

This approach might be considered obvious and time-consuming; thus, it is less structured in many organizations I have witnessed. Leaders have a key role in shaping the problem-solving culture in the organizations. Understanding and paying attention to the details may help reduce the chances of not having improvement initiatives viewed as quick wins, but rather as an integral part of a structured problem-solving approach. Heroic improvement simply cannot be realized without accountability and leadership engagement.

ROLE, ATTITUDE, BASIC SKILLS

Role

As a problem-solving facilitator, your role is to help leadership and to work with problem-solving teams to achieve desired outcomes. You may lead a team through problem-solving, but the purpose is to prepare the problem-solving team with a set of tools so they can eventually solve problems on their own. Also, you must create a safe work environment of respect for others, collaboration, learning experience, and growth. The objective is to build capability, transfer knowledge, and provide guidance to the leaders and problem-solving team to close the gap identified in the problem statement.

The leader is the sponsor individual in the organization who owns the problem and works closely with the facilitator to guide the execution of corrective actions. The leader is responsible for selecting the resources that will provide the problem-solving team with skills and knowledge. The leader is expected to welcome systems thinking, be an active resource for the problem-solving team, and spearhead the empowerment that will drive changes throughout the problem-solving process.

The problem-solving team members are responsible for executing assigned tasks diligently and to the highest standards by providing their knowledge, skills, time, and positive, open minds to adapting new ideas. It is expected that team members be outspoken by answering and escalating concerns, providing insight, and being able to contribute critical thinking.

Active engagement with leadership and the problem-solving team is the best way to set expectations, communicate, and disseminate information about the problem-solving approach and tools that will be used in a problem-solving initiative. This may be the hardest part of facilitating, especially in an environment where there is a lack of CI and problem-solving culture. For instance, you may find yourself in an environment where leadership and problem-solving teams are just in for quick wins. Then, you must acknowledge that you are dealing with individuals who easily lose sight of what is required to make and sustain changes. Does the leader have a firm grasp of the problem they want to solve? Does the leader understand the problem-solving approach and its phases? Does the leader acknowledge their role and the challenges that the problem-solving team is facing? Answering these questions can help you provide guidance to the leader, proactively avoiding any disruption to or detouring around the problem-solving process. You should be able to identify this kind of individual early in the game based on their behaviors. Some of these management behaviors include maintaining as much control as possible over the work output by micromanaging, jumping to conclusions without a thorough RCA, and reacting negatively to inputs and feedback.

Remember, your role is to make sure the expectations are set from the get-go and are top of mind for the sponsored leadership and the problem-solving team by conducting periodic check-ins.

A piece of advice is for you to identify a mechanism that works best to communicate effectively with leadership and/or the problem-solving team without losing sight of the problem-solving goal. The mechanism chosen must minimize the disruptive effects while ensuring continuous monitoring of all scheduled activities. Monitoring cross-functional activities is a pressing issue that challenges problem-solving practitioners to address change management as it affects communication. Therefore, visual systems are a strategy that can easily be adapted to maintain expectations at top of mind. This is an excellent tool that involves either direct human observation or automated data collection, allowing for complex information flow in a predictable manner and making progress visible. This is a storytelling system that provides clear feedback relative to expectations so that leadership can be aware of adjustments that can be made to achieve the problem-solving goal. Visual systems can be achieved by posting a tracking board with KPIs that measure against objectives and goals, such as gap to target, among others. You must make sure that leaders and the problem-solving team understand that a visual system is not to assign blame or to degrade a team that's struggling to meet their target. This is an effective way to visualize progress, identify areas that need to be escalated, and encourage others to help.

Lastly, the facilitator should always celebrate every team win and show gratitude for their hard work, acknowledging their contribution to achieving targets and goals. It is a simple gesture and a powerful motivator for individuals and teams.

Celebrating success authentically builds momentum and helps the team to continue to focus, delivering great results.

Attitude

The approach that you adapt as a problem-solving facilitator is key for your success as a facilitator. Respect for others is the fundamental essence of your approach. You'll be able to garner respect from others by listening and welcoming comments and inputs. At the same time, you must be rigorous in asking hard questions to seek information while ensuring a safe environment for the team to openly ask questions and share ideas and thoughts. On the other hand, if you tend to tell the problem-solving team what to do and how to do it, you will significantly impact your facilitation. Being aware of this tendency will help you adopt some flexibility where appropriate.

Asking yourself the following questions will help you enhance learning and develop self-awareness.

- What is my style of open communication channels? Do I make my team feel heard and respected?
- How do I manage providing objective feedback? What has been the impact on my team when I provide feedback?
- When is it appropriate to make decisions? How does the team react when I make the final decision?
- What are the implications of my facilitation style?
- What do I do to help retain employees? Do I inspire or motivate my team?
- Do I carry a positive attitude every day, all day?

It is normal to feel that you have fixed opinions about how things should be done and how your team should be managed. So, seeking a second set of eyes from your peers about your facilitating and leadership style helps you understand better how you perform. You cannot go wrong with getting insights into what you can do differently to improve. Your own attitude toward being open to active listening can increase your confidence. In my experience, adopting a positive attitude results in a better collaboration with the team and quality of work.

Remember that you are not the problem solver; the problem-solving team is responsible for solving the problem. You guide the team in using the tools. The people involved in the day-to-day job are accountable for finding sustainable solutions to their problems. As the facilitator, you are a listener and a sounding board, constantly challenging the thought process of the problem-solving team.

The facilitator strives to help the team to accurately identify, define, and reach a consensus on potential solutions. The facilitator must ensure that every team member participates in generating ideas, showing respect to each other, valuing other opinions, and listening carefully to other responses. An effective approach is to encourage the problem-solving team to discuss critical issues, not ignoring what is working well. During the discussion, the facilitator may encourage the team to consider ways to identify nonvalue-added activities. It is important to identify those individuals within the assigned problem-solving team who may have the knowledge and information required to fill the gap to solve a problem. On the other hand, the facilitator may identify the individuals who may resist changes. Resistance is usually created by uncertainty and lack of understanding; therefore, it is important for the facilitator to understand the nature of the resistance and how to get those individuals to actively provide feedback and add value to the problem-solving process.

How to deal with resistance to change

Resistance to change can be avoided if expectations are well set from the beginning. Resistance will always be present in any problem-solving initiative that you facilitate; it will not go away. However, there are many ways to mitigate people's pushbacks. An excellent facilitator communicates well, ensuring that there is no ambiguity or uncertainty. People will always resist the unknown, especially if they feel there is a threat of losing control of the authority they have. First, understand the origin of the resistance. *Why are people resisting? What do they know? What am I overlooking? What considerations are being left out? Are people on to something?*

When corrective actions include implementation of new technology, people will fear that their skill sets will no longer be needed or are obsolete. Certainly, new technologies and business intelligence are growing very fast and displacing people—this is a reality that we need to face. Facilitators must be honest and always talk truthfully about any implementation implications and consequences that could be a threat to the organization and its employees. Always telling the truth throughout the process will help you build a cohesive team. Demonstrating honesty is expected from every professional, and it will convey respect.

The effective facilitator is the one who listens well and exudes respect, imagination, technical expertise, experience, knowledge, credibility, leadership, influence, and awareness. These are desired attributes that will lead you toward success.

Basic Skills

Facilitating a problem-solving initiative is a complex task because you will deal with unpleasant situations, such as challenges, impasses, disagreements, and lack of accountability, among others. However, everybody is looking at the problem-solving facilitator as the individual with the silver bullet who will come up with the right solution that will please everyone, making things easy for others. A facilitator offers specific talents and the expertise to guide a team to solve a problem and to ensure that any changes implemented are sustained.

Facilitation is about learning about other people's thought processes so the facilitator can focus on how to provide better guidance to the problem-solving team. As we previously discussed, effective communication and listening are key attributes to being successful in terms of understanding how a team is reasoning. Once you understand how and why the problem-solving team is taking a specific approach to evaluate a situation, then you will be able to consider any facilitative forces that could be influencing your skills to provide better guidance.

A facilitator must possess the ability to think logically, and also be effective at decision-making and building teamwork. These skills will lead you to focus on a systematic analysis and approach for problem-solving, which encompasses everything covered in this book.

Start by reviewing in advance the problem the team wants to solve, and prepare questions to ask the team to discuss.

Depending on the scope of the problem, you plan the activities to ensure the following:

- Engage team members in brainstorming sessions, process mapping, workflow analysis, root cause analysis, process analysis, data analytics, developing corrective actions, and the validation process.
- Guide the problem-solving team outside their comfort zone.
- Provide process critique and feedback.
- Apply basic SPC concepts.
- Facilitate conversation with frontline individuals.

What are some of the skills a facilitator should have?

There are key skills and knowledge a problem-solving facilitator must have to achieve results through people: knowing the systematic process to solve any type of problem and building a connection and trust with the team. A facilitator will build trust by demonstrating knowledge and experience in the following areas:

- Analyzing business processes and workflows
- Data analytics
- Leveraging technology
- Working in a matrix organization
- Driving collaboration across businesses

+ Statistical process control
+ Continuous improvement process theory and practice
+ Coaching techniques
+ Project management techniques
+ Inspiring others
+ Written and verbal communication

FINAL THOUGHTS

Everybody has a hobby—mine is mountain biking. Throughout the years, I have tried various types of mountain bikes, and I remember in my early years riding a twenty-seven-speed bike, which is controlled by the gears located on the bike wheels and shifted with levers on the handlebars. The left lever controls three gears near the pedals, and the right lever controls nine gears on the back wheel, resulting in a twenty-seven-speed bike. The lowest gears help you sustain your energy longer while pedaling up steep inclines. Gears and shifters help you maintain cadence during your ride. However, finding a comfortable cadence by shifting gears to help you maintain speed is a challenge. New riders experience slips while trying to power uphill and changing gears when under heavy load; therefore, bikers must plan ahead and change into the right gear *before* hitting the hill.

Many organizations experience something similar to new riders when they learn that an improvement methodology is available and they try to implement it as a problem-solving approach. Oftentimes, when beginning their improvement journey, organizations start by identifying problems to solve. They begin with large initiatives and pull key staff away from their departments for long periods of time. Then, very soon they find out that the process repeatedly results in short-term gains and long-term sustainment of improvement initiatives that aren't achievable. Initiatives for improvements that began with support from upper management and teams faded after the initiative event, when the business rhythm or other crises developed and the attention shifted elsewhere. Therefore, it is highly recommended that each organization employ an experienced facilitator to provoke conversation on the problem that leaders want to solve. A facilitator will be able to identify the problem-solving team, create a stable workflow, and maintain cadence.

From experience, I have found many benefits to implementing a systematic approach to solving problems by starting small and getting individuals into the habit of thinking in systems. With a systematic approach, businesses can avoid individuals, leaders, employees, staff, or problem-solving teams from jumping to conclusions and offering what appears to be the obvious solution. Benefits also include understanding the business, as well as fostering problem-solving, improvement, and sustainment.

Understanding the Business

Listening to staff—and getting a solid understanding of their current work and processes—is critical in learning the business. In this way, leaders and direct reports are able to understand business priorities and processes, communication and information flow and daily constraints, and also exchange ideas about what is currently happening.

Empowering problem-solving

I like to empower staff with the ability to problem-solve, thus enabling them to own their challenges as they work to implement ideas and improvements. Keep in mind that staff closest to the job understand challenges best and how to overcome them. This is a great opportunity to get stakeholders engaged because corrective actions are getting traction in their daily work. Likewise, leadership must be engaged with and supportive of staff, but not impose solutions on them since, at the end of the day, the staff is the body accountable for the daily work.

Improvement

Optimizing processes and implementing a visual management system are key to keeping the business rhythm and observing how the organization adds value. Rather than improvising or shifting gears without a strategy for the work to be done, conduct weekly performance check-in meetings to encourage measuring performance indicators, reviewing outcomes, and force reflection around performance. These meetings must be designed to connect the improvements to the gap you desire to close. This allows for analysis and reflection on what it takes to achieve business results.

Sustainment

Managing processes in accordance with the standards is imperative to learn whether the standards produce the expected results. The sustainment of standards on current improvements provides a structure to have bidirectional communication of business strategy, goals, data, and results where information flows at each level of the organization from the executive management team to the staff, and vice versa.

I hope you can adopt a similar system to help solve problems and elucidate complex problems and recurring challenges that impede your staff, performance, and business growth. However, the four areas covered in this book—UNDERSTANDING, SYSTEMATIC PROBLEM-SOLVING, IMPROVEMENT, and SUSTAINMENT—are mutually exclusive and would not have the same performance impact if one was excluded. Just like managing a mountain bike gearing system, understanding the ideal cadence for various conditions affects the riding performance. A higher cadence on a lower gear is more efficient than pedaling slower in a harder gear.

About the Author

Rolando A. Berríos is a professional engineer with over 20 years of experience in systems optimization and operational excellence. He applies methods from management science—such as applied statistics, data analytics, and operation research—to develop process models that help businesses make better decisions. Rolando developed his problem-solving skills by working in a wide variety of organizations, including government, supply chain, health care, construction, manufacturing, and telecommunication. He holds a Doctor of Philosophy degree in Systems Engineering, a Master of Sciences degree in Economics, and a bachelor's degree in Industrial & Systems Engineering and Civil Engineering.

Printed in Great Britain
by Amazon